FROM HELLA TO HYPHY

FROM HELLA TO HYPHY

The Bay Area Slang Dictionary

Standard Edition

FROM HELLA TO HYPHY

Copyright © 2026 Firstclass Media

ALL RIGHTS RESERVED

No part of this publication may be reproduced, distributed, or transmitted in any form or by any means, including photocopying, recording, or other electronic or mechanical methods, without the prior written permission of the publisher, except in the case of brief quotations used in reviews or scholarly works.

For permission requests, write to the publisher at:
thefirstclassmediagroup@gmail.com

ISBN: 979-8-9933178-1-6

First Edition

Cover and interior design by Eryc Parnell Fields

Printed in the United States of America

Dedicated

to

Mil-Ticket

Always & Forever
Town Business

CONTENTS

Introduction 1
How to Use This Book 3

Dictionary

0–9 5
A 8
B 14
C 43
D 60
E 77
F 80
G 99
H 119
I 136
J 144
K 147
L 152
M 166
N 180
O 186
P 201
Q 221
R 222
S 231
T 272
U 292
V 295
W 296
Y 310
Z 320

Appendices

Thematic Index 322
About the Publisher 325

INTRODUCTION

From *Hella to Hyphy* is a journey into one of the richest cultures in America — the vocabulary of the Bay Area! Language here has never been "just words." It reflects survival, creativity, and change. But the Bay gave the world more than music, technology, and movements. It gave us expressions that traveled far beyond Oakland, San Francisco, and San Jose, shaping hip-hop, pop culture, and everyday conversation across the globe. Words like *Hater, Hyphy,* and, of course, *Hella* didn't just end up in the dictionary by accident. They were born here, on these streets, in these neighborhoods, and in the voices of the people. It's the language of *game,* and in the Bay Area, *game* is more than a word — it's a way of life.

The Bay Area is one of the most diverse places in the country. Oakland is the most diverse city in America, with no single group being the majority. That mix of cultures alone would create interesting language. But the Bay also sits at the center of movements that shaped America: the Black Panther Party was born in Oakland in 1966, teaching people to stand up for themselves, and that pride still shows in how people here move and talk. The decades that followed saw Oakland develop its own street culture and vocabulary that spread into everyday speech. Meanwhile, the local hip-hop scene refused to copy East Coast or West Coast trends, instead sharing homegrown slang with the world.

These forces didn't just coexist. They collided, merged, and produced something unique: a vocabulary unlike any other in the world — one that speaks to history, identity, and respect.

Slang has the power to do more than describe. It connects. It bridges generations between parents and children, teachers and students. It gives newcomers a way to belong and locals a reason to stand taller in their pride. It helps visitors understand that when they set foot here, they're entering a place with its own heartbeat, its own code, and its own language.

This book doesn't shy away from debate. Who coined what? How should it be used? Where do credit and appreciation collide? Those conversations are part of the legacy too.

So as you turn these pages, don't just read the words — listen to the voices behind them. Feel the pride of a region that takes its language seriously. Recognize the influence of Oakland, a city whose history runs from the Black Panther Party to independent hip-hop, from sideshows to Silicon Valley. Discover the answers to local mysteries: does food slap or smack? (It smacks; music slaps, don't let anyone tell you different.) And above all, celebrate the creativity of a people who turned everyday talk into something recognized around the world.

This is the language. This is the Bay.
This is From Hella to Hyphy.

HOW TO USE THIS BOOK

Entry Structure

Each entry in this dictionary follows a consistent format to help you quickly find and understand Bay Area slang terms:

Entry Word — The term appears in bold blue text at the top of each entry.

Pronunciation — A phonetic guide shows how the word is spoken.

Part of Speech — Indicates whether the term is a noun, verb, adjective, phrase, etc.

Definition — A clear explanation of what the term means and how it's used.

Sidebars

Some entries include additional context in colored sidebars:

Blue sidebar — Etymology and historical background, explaining where the term came from and how it evolved.

Gold sidebar — Example sentences showing the term used in authentic context.

See Also — Cross-references to related terms appear in gray italic at the bottom of entries.

Special Entries

Nine terms receive expanded coverage as standalone features due to their cultural significance: Billy Doo, Game, Hella, Hyphy, The Hyphy Movement, Mobb Music, Player, Player Hater, and Sideshow. These entries include deeper historical context and cultural analysis.

Thematic Index

The back of the book includes a Thematic Index that groups terms by category, such as Music & Sound, Money & Finance, Vehicles & Transportation, and more. Use this index to explore related terms or to find words when you know the general topic but not the specific term.

A Note on Language

This dictionary documents language as it is actually used. Some terms may be considered offensive, explicit, or controversial. Their inclusion reflects their cultural significance and real-world usage, not endorsement. Where terms contain explicit language, partial censoring (such as s***) is used.

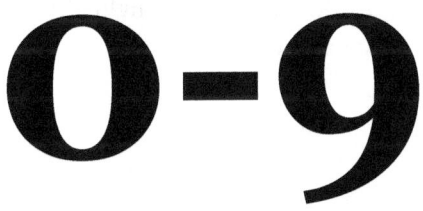

2 On The 10

/too awn thuh ten/
(phrase)

To exaggerate or overstate, often to make oneself appear more impressive, important, or affected than they actually are. Typically used to call out someone for making something seem more dramatic than it was.

> "You know it ain't even go down like that so quit putin' the 2 on the 10."

(See also: High Power, Lie To Kick It, Put It On Thick)

4 15's

/fohr fif-teenz/
(noun)

A popular car audio setup in old school Bay Area car culture, consisting of four 15-inch woofers installed in the trunk to produce powerful bass output.

> "Bruh Chev was slappin' hella hard, he must've had 4 15's in that thang."

(See also: Bump, Knock, Slap)

4 Much

/foh much/
(phrase)

A play on "too much," used to describe behavior that is worse than excessive, exaggerated, or unnecessarily dramatic. Often highlights actions that go far beyond what is reasonable or expected.

> "Bruh actin' like she his wife already. He doin' 4 much."

(See also: Doin' Too Much, Extra, Extra'd Out)

5-O

/faiyv-oh/
(noun)

The police.

> "Soon as we seen 5-O hit the block we got little."

(See also: Po Po, Task, The Boys, The Rollers)

10 Toes Down

/ten tohz down/
(phrase)

Complete dedication, loyalty, or commitment to a person, principle, or situation, especially in the face of adversity.

> "When everything went left bruh stayed 10 toes down."

(See also: Solid)

16

/six-teen/
(noun)

A coded reference to the letter P, the 16th letter of the alphabet. Used to refer to a pimp or player.

> *"She a 3-0-4 so you already know, she need a real 16."*

(See also: "P")

18 Dummy

/ay-teen dum-ee/
(verb phrase)

Used to describe something reaching an extreme or intense level, especially in the context of energy, excitement, or crowd reaction. Commonly associated with the hyphy movement.

> *Sometimes shortened to "18."*
>
> *"Soon as the beat dropped, they went 18 dummy."*

(See also: Dummy, Go Dumb, Hyphy)

42 Fake

/for-tee-too fayk/
(noun)

A deceptive move or fake out, often used to mislead or outsmart someone. The phrase is styled to sound like a football play, emphasizing misdirection.

> *"Bruh 42 faked em and got up outta there."*

A Lil Bit Of Nothin'
/uh lil bit uh nuth-in/
(phrase)

Purchased cheap, or at a good or low price.

> "He shot me the player price on the Camaro; got it for a lil bit a nothin'."

(See also: Player Price)

A.O.B.
/ay-oh-bee/
(initialism, noun)

An initialism for "All On a B****," referring to a situation where a woman pays for or provides something, often used in pimp culture to highlight that her resources covered the expense.

> "You already know, it's A.O.B. wit me."

A1
/ay-wuhn/
(adjective)

A term used to describe a car modification where the front of the vehicle is lifted higher than the back, causing it to sit at an angle. By extension, it can describe anything positioned or styled at a noticeable tilt.

> Derived from A1 Springs, a suspension shop in Oakland, CA, founded in 1950.

> "He got the drop 'stang wit thangs, bump, and it's sittin' A1."

A1 Yola

/ay-wuhn yoh-luh/
(noun)

High-quality cocaine.

> *Often shortened to just "yola," itself a phonetic alteration of "cola" (as in Coca-Cola), a colloquialism for cocaine derived from "coke."*
>
> *"He out there slangin' that A1 Yola, no soda."*

(See also: Cola, Cream)

Actin' Funny

/ak-tin fun-ee/
(phrase)

Behaving in a stingy or ungenerous manner, particularly when someone is reluctant to share with others.

> *"She came through and snatched me every day last week, but now she actin' funny with the rides."*

(See also: Bootsie, Skantless)

Active

/ak-tiv/
(adjective)

Currently participating in street activity, especially involving crime, violence, or the drug trade.

> *"After all these years, bruh still active."*

(See also: In The Field)

Ain't Even Cool

/aynt ee-vin kool/
(phrase)

Spoken with disappointment when someone or something lets you down, or with judgment when a person gives off the wrong kind of energy, or something just doesn't sit right. Used to emphasize that it was not cool at all; not right, not enjoyable, not even close, etc. The emphasis falls on *even*, highlighting how far off it felt.

> *Sometimes styled in the past tense as "wasn't even cool."*
>
> *"It end up bein' all bad for real. It wasn't even cool."*

Ain't S***

/aynt s***/
(phrase)

A casual response indicating that nothing important is happening or that everything is routine. Often used to downplay activity or avoid giving detail.

> *Sometimes shortened to just "s***."*
>
> *"What's up wit blood?" "Ain't s***."*

Aired Out

/aird owt/
(verb)

Hit with a barrage of gunfire, typically from an automatic or assault-style weapon. Often refers to a person, vehicle, or location being riddled with bullets.

> "They caught him at the light and aired out the whole whip."

(See also: Lit Up)

All Day

/awl day/
(verb)

A term referring to a life sentence in prison.

> "They snatched bruh up for that hot one. They gave him all day."

(See also: Kickstand, Washed)

All Gas No Brakes

/awl gas no brayks/
(phrase)

Moving forward with full intensity, effort, and determination, without hesitation or restraint. Often used to describe relentless ambition, energy, or drive in pursuit of a goal.

> "I took a setback, but I'm about to make a comeback. It's all gas, no brakes."

All Geezus

/awl jee-zus/
(expression)

A stylized variation of All G (short for "All Good"), used to express that everything is fine or there's no issue. Often said in response to a favor, mistake, or minor offense, it reflects cool-headedness and ease. Plays off the phonetic sound of "G," extending it into Geezus for added flavor and personality.

> "I'm on my way to swoop you, be ready." "It's All Geezus."

(See also: It's All Good)

All The S***

/awl thuh s***/
(phrase)

Refers to everything without limitation, implying that nothing is off limits or that all options are available. Often used to express readiness, capability, or openness to any and all actions or experiences.

> "Tell bruh bring the bottles, the girls, all the s***."

(See also: Errythang)

All To The Good

/awl tuh thuh good/
(phrase)

Essentially another way of saying It's all good, used to express that a situation is fine, acceptable, or without issue.

> The phrase is sometimes shortened in speech to "it's to the good."

> "Don't trip, bruh. It's all to the good."

(See also: It's All Good)

Alright Then
/aw-rite den/
(phrase)

A casual farewell or goodbye.

> "Alright then, I'ma holla at you in a minute."

(See also: Be Smooth, In A Minute, Love Your Life)

Aunt Clara
/ahnt klair-uh/
(noun)

A joking nickname for the AC Transit bus line, playing on the initials "A.C."

> "I missed my ride, so I had to catch Aunt Clara to work."

Ayyy
/ay/
(interjection)

An expressive slang term used to convey excitement, surprise, or enthusiasm. It can also be a greeting or a way to draw attention to a moment or statement.

> "Ayyy, what's good wit it!"

(See also: Yeee!)

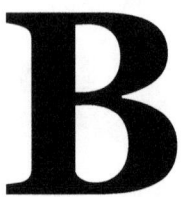

B-Town
/bee town/
(noun)

A nickname for Berkeley, California, often used with local pride or territorial reference.

> *"I'm hollerin' at a bad lil thang from B-Town."*

Baby Girl
/bay-bee gurl/
(noun)

A casual or affectionate term used to address a woman, often in a flirtatious, persuasive, or familiar tone. May be used to soften a request, get someone's attention, or simply as part of conversational style, regardless of context.

> *"Baby girl, check it out one time."*

(See also: Lil Mama)

Ballin'
/baw-lin/
(verb)

Living lavishly or possessing wealth; doing extremely well financially.

> *"Unk a real factor out here, he been ballin' since the 70's."*

(See also: Banked Up, Caked Up, Gettin' It, Havin' It, On, Papered Up)

Ballin' Out Of Control

/baw-lin owt uh cun-trohl/
(phrase)

Having an extraordinary amount of wealth, often accumulated rapidly.

> "Bruh got a house on the hill and four foreign whips, he ballin' outta control."

(See also: Ballin', Banked Up, Caked Up, Gettin' It, Havin' It, On, Papered Up)

Balloons To A Blimp

/buh-loonz tuh uh blimp/
(phrase)

Used to emphasize how minor or insignificant something is in comparison to one's capabilities or stature, suggesting it's hardly worth their attention or consideration.

> "It's nothin' to a boss, ya understand me? It's balloons to a blimp, mayne!"

(See also: It's Nothin', Peanuts To An Elephant, Small Thing To A Giant)

Bammer

/bam-er/
(noun)

Low-quality marijuana, typically considered weak, harsh, or lacking potency.

> "We had to smoke five blunts just to feel it, straight bammer."

Band

/band/
(noun)

One thousand dollars. Often heard in the plural as bandz, where it can also mean money in larger sums more generally.

> "I got a band say the Warriors beat the brakes off the Lakers."
>
> "He pulled up in the Benz with ten bandz in his lap."

(See also: Bandaid, Rack, Thou-Wow)

Bandaid

/ban-dayd/
(noun)

A variant of band, also meaning one thousand dollars.

> Derived from the paper wraps (bands) banks use to wrap currency.
>
> "If I'ma have to do all that, I'ma need a bandaid."

(See also: Band, Rack, Thou-Wow)

Banger

/bang-er/
(noun)

A song with strong energy, standout appeal, or heavy production, often considered a hit. Can also refer to a firearm, especially in casual or street contexts.

> "Bruh, that new joint a banger."
>
> "He got caught with the banger on him."

(See also: Hammer, Thang, Thumper)

Bank

/bangk/
(noun, verb)

Refers to money, especially in large amounts; commonly used to highlight financial success or wealth. Also used as a verb meaning to hit or punch someone, typically in a confrontational context.

> "He on his third business. That boy havin' bank."
>
> "I'm bout to bank on you."

(See also: Mail, Paper, Skrilla)

Banked On

/bainkt awn/
(verb phrase)

To have been hit or attacked; the past tense of Bank in this context.

> "Keep talkin', you gon get banked on."

(See also: Fired On, Stole On, Take Off)

Banked Up

/bainkt uhp/
(adjective)

Having a lot of money; indicates substantial wealth or financial success.

> "After that last deal, he all the way banked up."

(See also: Ballin', Gettin' It, Havin' It)

Bap

/bap/
(verb)

To crash, wreck, or fall hard.

> "He was lookin' back at that girl and damn near bapped the Chev."

(See also: Scrub)

Barz

/barz/
(noun)

A high level of skill or ability, indicating control. Typically used in reference to driving, cutting hair, or other hands-on activities requiring precision or coordination.

> Likely derived from "handlebars."

> "He got barz wit the clippers."

(See also: Handles)

Bay Boy

/bay boi/
(noun)

A male from the Bay Area. The term is both a regional identifier and a playful twist on Playboy, often used with pride or swagger to highlight someone's Bay roots and character.

> "He been a Bay Boy since the jump, you can hear it in how he talk."

(See also: Baydestrian)

Bay Luv

/bay luhv/
(expression)

A show of mutual respect or appreciation between individuals from the Bay Area, often acknowledging shared roots, loyalty, or support. Commonly used when showing love to someone from the Bay, especially while out of town. Can also refer to love shown by a Bay native to someone from outside the community, expressed in a Bay-centric and uniquely recognizable way.

> *"Good lookin', bruh. Straight Bay luv, on my mama."*

Baydestrian

/bay-dess-tree-uhn/
(noun, adjective)

A native or resident of the Bay Area. Often used with pride to signal regional identity, cultural fluency, or a strong connection to Bay Area language, style, and lifestyle. The term can also describe a perspective or way of thinking that reflects Bay Area values, humor, or attitude.

> *"You already know how I move. I'm a real Baydestrian."*

BD

/bee-dee/
(initialism, noun)

Initialism for "Baby Daddy"; the father of one's child, often no longer a formal partner. Commonly used informally or in casual conversation.

> *"She say she waitin' on her BD to drop some money off."*

(See also: BM)

Be Smooth
/bee smoov/
(phrase)

A casual farewell; akin to "take care" or "be safe."

> "Alright, I'll see you later, bra; be smooth."

(See also: Alright Then, In A Minute, Love Your Life)

Beat
/beet/
(noun)

Refers to the sound system in a car, often emphasizing bass and volume. Can also refer to a song that is especially good or has strong musical appeal. Less commonly, can be used as slang for intercourse.

> "Bra pulled up in the old school wit hella beat."

> "That's the beat right there."

(See also: Banger, Bump, Knock, Slap)

Beezy
/bee-zee/
(noun)

A coded or softened term used in place of various words for a woman that begin with the letter "b." Commonly used in casual or informal conversation, often to reference a woman without using harsher language.

> "The lil beezy kept blowin' up my phone last night."

(See also: Breezy)

Belushi
/buh-loo-shee/
(noun)

A mixture of cocaine and heroin.

> *Named after actor John Belushi, who died from a fatal overdose of the combination.*
>
> *"That Belushi got bra out here actin' mainy."*

Bend
/bend/
(noun)

To turn the corner or circle the block while driving.

> *"Bend the block so we could highside on em one time."*

Bent

/bent/
(adjective)

Used to express that someone has you confused, misjudged, or misunderstood in a way that violates, oversteps, or encroaches upon personal boundaries or values.

> *Also used as the plural of "bend."*
>
> *Often phrased as "got me bent" to emphasize disbelief or defiance in response to someone's words or actions.*
>
> *"We bent the corner on gold ones, lookin' saucy."*
>
> *"You talkin' reckless like I ain't gon say nothin'; you got me bent, blud."*

(See also: Twisted)

Bet Not

/bed-not/
(verb phrase)

An abbreviated form of better not, used as a warning, caution, or strong suggestion against doing something.

> *Sometimes phrased as "best not."*
>
> *"You bet not be late again."*

Big Bruh

/big bruh/
(noun)

A term of respect for an older male associate, usually someone close in age who plays a big brother or mentor role. Occasionally used toward a younger man or peer in a way that reflects submission, insecurity, or a lack of self-respect, often because of money or perceived status.

> "These suckas will call a baby 'Big Bruh' if he got some money."

(See also: O.G.)

Big Thang

/big thayng/
(noun)

A large firearm, usually a fully automatic rifle.

> "Blud jumped out wit that big thang, he was not playin'."

(See also: Thang)

Bip

/bip/
(verb)

The act of breaking a car window in order to steal the contents inside.

> "Don't park the whip downtown bra, you liable to get bipped."

(See also: Lick)

BILLY DOO

A well-known figure in Oakland's local mythology, spoken of as a menacing presence in and around Arroyo Park. Said to have stalked and assaulted children after dark, Billy Doo (sometimes spelled *Dew*) became Oakland's "Boogie Man"; a symbol of fear and terror for generations of locals.

Descriptions vary. Some recall a tall, slender, dark-skinned Black man, rumored to be a former track star. Others describe him as a stocky, mixed-race man with short, nappy hair.

Though never officially documented, the legend of Billy Doo remains embedded in East Oakland's oral history as both a warning and a symbol of caution.

Blade

/blayd/
(noun)

A known area or strip where prostitution activity takes place. Can also refer to someone who is gay or homosexual.

> "The blade was rollin' last night."

Blap

/blap/
(noun, verb)

A phonetic variation of Slap, used to describe music that hits hard, particularly with heavy bass. Used interchangeably with Slap in reference to songs or sound systems.

> *Potentially a fusion of "bump" and "slap."*
>
> "This beat straight blap."

(See also: Beat, Bump, Knock, Slap)

Bless

/bles/
(verb)

To do a favor for someone, offer a gift, or extend a gesture of generosity, often providing more than what is owed or expected.

> "Auntie filled my whole plate. I wasn't even hungry like that, but she blessed me."

(See also: Hooked, Joog, Plug)

Blow Up
/bloh uhp/
(verb)

To leave a relationship abruptly, often without warning or justification; commonly used when referring to a prostitute walking away from her situation. Can also mean to call or contact someone excessively.

> "He was really feelin' lil mama; that was a bad blow up."
>
> "I told you I was busy, baby; quit blowin' me up."

(See also: Fag Off, Hit My Line)

Blud
/bluhd/
(noun)

A casual, familiar form of address similar to *bruh*, most commonly heard in Oakland. Spoken casually among peers, especially in conversations with a local edge.

> Derived from "youngblood."
>
> Spelling is intentional; not to be confused with b-l-o-o-d.
>
> Perhaps the primary form of address in Oakland, later succeeded by "potna," and eventually "bruh."
>
> "Blud and them out there doin' the damn thang."

(See also: Bruh, Potna)

Blueberries & Cherries

/bloo-bair-eez and chair-eez/
(noun)

A phrase referring to the red and blue lights of a police vehicle, especially when seen flashing in the rearview mirror during a traffic stop.

> "I got jacked by 5-0, all I seen was blueberries & cherries."

(See also: Blurped, Jacked)

Blurped

/blurrpt/
(verb)

Being pulled over by the police.

> *Derived from the sound of a short police siren.*
>
> "I got blurped on Foothill."

(See also: Blueberries & Cherries, Jacked)

BM

/bee-em/
(initialism, noun)

Short for "Baby's Momma" or "Baby's Mother." The mother of one's child, often no longer a formal partner.

> "I need to go drop this money off to my BM right quick."

Bo

/bo/
(suffix, noun)

A suffix added to the end of a male's first name or nickname. Especially common in Oakland, it modifies a name to create a distinctive tone or identity. Likely derived from "boy," the suffix reflects a regional style of name construction rooted in local expression. Separately, bo is also used as a street term for prescription-strength cough syrup. It typically refers to syrups containing promethazine and codeine, often used recreationally.

> *Originally derived from robitussin but later applied more broadly.*
> *"Relly-Bo been solid since day one. You already know what he on."*
> *"Bruh over there off that bo. He in slow motion right now."*

Bolo

/boh-loh/
(adjective, adverb)

Phonetic alteration of "solo," used to describe being single, unaccompanied, or alone. Often said when someone is moving by themselves or doing something without company, and often used in conjunction with solo as in solo-bolo, or possibly as an abbreviation of it.

> *"I pullt up to the function bolo."*

(See also: To The Face, To The Neck)

Bomb

/bahm/
(noun)

High-quality marijuana. Also used for heroin.

> *"That boi over there loaded off that bomb."*

(See also: Dank, Gas, Good, Nade)

Boo Thang

/boo thayng/
(noun)

A romantic partner or love interest, often used playfully or affectionately to describe someone you're dating, in love with, or emotionally attached to. Can apply to both serious relationships and flirty situationships.

> *"That's my lil boo thang tho, don't get it twisted."*
>
> *"He popped out with his new lil boo thang at the function."*

Bookin'

/book-in/
(verb)

Running fast, usually in a hurry or with urgency.

> *"Soon as the bell rang, they was bookin' to the bus stop."*

(See also: Burl, Hully, Strike)

Boop, Bop

/boop, bop/
(interjection)

A set of onomatopoeic sound effects imitating the rhythm or impact of punches. Commonly used in storytelling, or casual speech to dramatize the act of hitting someone. The playful sounds emphasize action while keeping the description light or exaggerated.

> *Sometimes phrased as "boop, bip."*
>
> *"Gave blud the two-piece, like boop, bop, it was over just that quick."*

(See also: Fired On, Leaked, Stole On)

Bootsie

/boot-see/
(adjective)

Something or someone considered undesirable, whether in style, behavior, or situation.

> *"Bruh wore some extra bootsie shoes to the function."*
>
> *"They laid him off right before the holidays; hella bootsie."*

(See also: Bunk, Janky)

Bopper

/bop-er/
(noun)

A woman perceived as promiscuous or eager for attention from multiple men.

> *Sometimes shortened to "Bop."*
>
> *"She ain't never been loyal a day in her life; she a straight bop."*

(See also: Fluker, Ripper, Runner)

Boss

/baws/
(noun)

A person who is in charge, a leader, or someone top-tier in status. Can also refer to oral sex, especially in casual or coded conversation.

> *"He move like a boss, real calculated wit it."*
>
> *"She just gave him some boss and dipped."*

Boss Up

/baws uhp/
(verb phrase)

To rise to a challenge with confidence, often by stepping into a higher level of responsibility, control, or maturity. Often refers to handling a situation decisively or assertively, especially in a way that earns respect, by elevating one's mindset or actions.

> *"He bossed up and paid for the whole meal."*
>
> *"I had to boss up and handle that."*

Bounce

/bowns/
(verb)

To leave or depart from a place. Can also refer to moving with energy or spring, such as waking up, getting active, or entering a vehicle.

> "The party was gettin' weak, so I had to bounce."
>
> "I just bounced up, what's the move for today?"

(See also: Dip, Do It Movin', Shake The Spot, Spin Off, Tucked)

Bounce Out

/bowns owt/
(verb phrase)

To exit a vehicle, often with a sense of urgency or purpose. This term can imply readiness for action, in both confrontational and non-confrontational contexts, and is frequently used to describe a dynamic or sudden movement.

> "She bounced out the car lookin' hella thick."

Bout That Action

/bowt that ak-shun/
(phrase)

Ready to act rather than talk. Implies being prepared, decisive, and consistently down for whatever situation arises, with a no-nonsense attitude and a reputation for following through.

> Sometimes abbreviated as "BTA."
>
> "I don't be doin' all that talkin'; I'm just bout that action, boss."

(See also: Get Active)

Boy
/boi/
(noun)

A term used to signify someone who is highly respected or official in street culture; often referring to individuals with status, wealth, or reputation, particularly in drug dealing or violent activity.

> *Also stylized as "boi."*
>
> *Frequently preceded by "real" for emphasis.*
>
> *"You might don't wanna test bra pimpin', he a real boy out here."*

(See also: Factor, Major Factor)

The Boys
/thuh boyz/
(noun)

A colloquial term referring to the police or law enforcement.

> *"The boys just slid through, we gotta dip."*

(See also: 5-O, Po Po, The Rollers, Task)

Break

/brayk/
(verb)

To take all of someone's money or resources, whether given up voluntarily, lost through competition, or taken through persuasion or force. Also used to mean taking off running, often suddenly or without warning, usually to avoid danger, confrontation, or capture.

> *"If you ain't got no game, she'll break you for everythang you got."*
>
> *"Soon as they slid through, everybody broke."*

(See also: Break Bread, Burl)

Break Bread

/brayk bred/
(verb phrase)

A request for payment, for someone to spend money, or to handle a financial obligation. Can refer to paying a debt, making a purchase, or covering a cost.

> *"You got my money? Break Bread or fake dead."*

(See also: Cash Me Out, Kick Me Down, Run Mine)

Breathin'
/breeth-in/
(verb)

To talk excessively in an uninhibited way, whether by speaking on unnecessary subjects, revealing sensitive information, lying, or otherwise going on longer than needed. The term often carries a negative tone, calling out someone for running their mouth too much.

> "Bruh stay breathin' about stuff that don't even matter."

(See also: Givin' Up Game, Jawsin', Put It On Thick, Wolfin')

Breezy
/bree-zee/
(noun)

A casual variation of "broad," used to refer to a woman. Also used to describe someone who appears smooth, stylish, or well put-together in an effortless way. Often said with admiration or flair.

> "He always got a new breezy ridin' wit him."
> "That jacket wet bra, you breezy."

(See also: Beezy, Clean, Fitted, Saucy)

Brody
/broh-dee/
(noun)

A casual variation of "brother," used to refer to a male friend or associate.

> "What's good, brody?"

(See also: Brother, Bruh)

Brother

/bruh-ther/
(noun)

Similar in meaning to bra, breh, or bruh, but intentionally pronounced in full with a hard "-er" at the end. Considered Bay-specific slang because it's said properly on purpose, often delivered quickly, with the speed of utterance itself being part of the style. This contrasts the more common shortened forms. Often used for emphasis, sarcasm, or to make a point, and sometimes reserved for close friends to underscore familiarity or respect.

> "What you got going on today, brother?"

(See also: Bruh)

Brought Back

/brawt bak/
(verb phrase)

Restored to former glory or optimal standards. Often used to describe anything refreshed or improved, such as a fresh haircut, a vehicle restoration, or the revival of something that had fallen off in quality or appearance.

> Sometimes phrased as "brung back."
> Related to the phrase "brought back from the dead."
> "Bruh brought you back; that cut hella clean."

Bruh

/bruh/
(noun)

A colloquial variation of bro or brother, characteristic of the conversational style in the Oakland Bay Area.

> The form bruh is frequently repeated for emphasis, as in "bruh bruh."
>
> Alternate spellings include "bra" and "breh," with "breh" reflecting a slightly different pronunciation.
>
> "Good seein' you, bruh, tap in."

(See also: Blud, Brother, Potna)

Bubble

/buh-buhl/
(verb)

To grow or build wealth, often by reinvesting profits to increase one's position or status. In street contexts, refers to flipping an investment, such as a wholesale drug buy, to generate more profit, similar in sentiment to come up.

> "I need a double-up so I can bubble up."

(See also: Come Up, Double Up, Stack)

Bucket

/buk-it/
(noun)

An old, beat-up, or mechanically deficient car.

> "If she can't ride in the bucket, she can't ride in the Benz."

(See also: Mobby)

Buff

/buff/
(noun)

To harshly reprimand or verbally discipline someone, often in response to major mistakes or serious rule-breaking. The term can also refer to giving a compliment with ulterior motives, often as a psychological tactic or setup for a later request, or describe something visually impressive, especially flashy or diamond-studded jewelry.

> *The reprimand usage is primarily associated with Richmond, CA and the surrounding West Contra Costa area (West Country).*
>
> "You already know moms finna buff you when you get home."
>
> "He tried to buff her with compliments before askin' for the favor."

(See also: Bussin', Check)

Bump

/buhmp/
(noun, verb)

Refers to the deep, bass-heavy sound from a car stereo or the act of playing loud music that emphasizes bass. Can also describe a song with a strong beat that hits hard or stands out.

> "Blud got hella bump in the old school."
>
> "They was bumpin' all through the town."

(See also: Beat, Knock, Pound, Slap, Subin')

Bumpin' Ya Gums

/bump-in yuh gumz/
(phrase)

Speaking excessively, often without purpose or much thought; running your mouth.

> Sometimes shortened or phrased as "bumpin' 'em."
>
> "You can't really listen to bruh, blud just be bumpin' his gums."

(See also: Jawsin')

Bundle

/bun-duhl/
(noun)

A bag of drugs intended for sale.

> "Big homie shot me a 300 bundle, I'm gettin' twenty off the hunnid."

Bunk

/buhngk/
(adjective)

Used to describe something weak, subpar, or disappointing in quality.

> "That new spot everybody hyped up was straight bunk."

(See also: Bootsie)

The Burg

/thuh burg/
(noun)

Pittsburg, California. A locally recognized shorthand used mostly by nearby Bay Area residents.

> "We slid out to The Burg after the game."

Burl

/burl/
(verb)

To run or move quickly.

> *Possibly derived from "burrow" or just a sound-alike.*
>
> "When I was little we seen Billy Doo at the creek, we had to burl."

Burners

/burn-erz/
(noun)

Snug-fitting leather gloves with knuckle holes and wrist straps, often worn as a sign of toughness, indicating a readiness to engage in physical confrontation.

> "When bra took them burners out his back pocket, you already knew what time it was."

Buss A B****

/bus uh b****/
(verb phrase)

To make a U-turn while driving.

> "Pull up to the intersection and buss a b****, bruh."

(See also: U-ey)

Bussin'

/buss-in/
(adjective)

Impressively good in appearance or style; stands out noticeably in a positive way. Often said about jewelry, clothing, cars, or anything visually striking.

> "That watch lightweight bussin', breh."

(See also: Clean, Saucy)

Busta

/buh-stuh/
(noun)

Someone considered cowardly, fake, or lacking respect. Used as a general insult for a person viewed as soft, disloyal, or untrustworthy.

> "Bruh switched up when things got tough; straight busta."

(See also: Mark, Perpetrator, Sucka)

But Now
/but now/
(phrase)

Used to pivot or reinforce a statement. A transitional phrase that underscores contrast, contradiction, or continuation, similar in spirit to "even so," "however," or "regardless."

> "My squad lost the game, but now, it's all good."

Bwoi
/bwoiah/
(noun)

A Bay Area variation of "boy," with a pronunciation almost exclusive to Oakland and the East Bay. Often used at the end of sentences as a casual term of address for a young man, similar to bro or dude.

> "What's up, bwoi?"

(See also: Blud, Bruh)

B'La
/bee-lah/
(noun)

An extended blunt created by connecting two or more blunt papers end to end.

> Named after and likely originated by Bay Area rapper B-Legit.
>
> "We twisted up a hunnid dolla B'La for the concert."

Caked Up
/kaykt uhp/
(phrase)

Having a lot of money; financially well-off.

> "He used to be broke, but now he out here caked up."

(See also: Ballin', Banked Up, Gettin' It, Havin' It, On, Papered Up)

Cannon
/kan-in/
(noun)

A large handgun.

> "He ain't tryin' to fight, bruh got a cannon on him."

(See also: Hammer, Thang, Thumper)

Cap
/kap/
(verb)

To jokingly insult or tease someone in a playful way, much like roasting or playing the dozens.

> *The exaggeration and embellishment essential to effective capping is the connective tissue to today's "no cap" and "that's cap."*
>
> "We would always have a cap contest on the bus after practice."

(See also: Clown, Whoride)

Capped On
/kappt awn/
(verb phrase)

To have been insulted in a joking way.

> "Soon as she hit the door he capped on her hella hard."

Captain
/kap-tin/
(noun)

A shortened form of Captain Save-A-Hoe, used to describe a man who defends, protects, or caters to a woman in a way seen as excessive, unnecessary, or undeserved. The term often implies misplaced effort or intervention beyond what is considered reasonable or respected.

> "Boss up one time and quit bein' a captain!"

(See also: Savin')

Cash Me Out
/kash mee owt/
(phrase)

A request to be paid.

> "You know you lost that bet, bruh; go on and cash me out."

(See also: Break Bread, Kick Me Down, Run Mine)

Cash Out

/kash owt/
(verb phrase)

To spend money, often in large amounts or on significant purchases. Can also refer generally to making a purchase, or payment.

> "Bruh cashed out on a new whip last week."

(See also: Cash Me Out)

Cat

/kat/
(noun, verb)

A shortened form of *J Cat*, used to describe someone acting foolishly, irrationally, or inconsistently. Can also refer to behavior marked by unreliability, such as ducking responsibility, showing up late, or failing to follow through.

> "You can't really depend on bra, blud's a cat."

(See also: Cat Off, J Cat)

Cat Off

/kat awf/
(verb phrase)

Wasting time or acting foolishly, associated with the terms *J Cat* or *Cat*, both of which denote erratic or irrational behavior.

> "Stop cattin' off and get to work."

(See also: Cat, J Cat)

Caught Slippin'
/kawt slip-in/
(phrase)

Being taken advantage of or suffering consequences due to lack of awareness, attention or preparation.

> "I got caught slippin' last week, they peelt me for errythang."

Cavi
/cav-ee/
(noun)

A laced marijuana cigarette mixed with cocaine.

> Sometimes pronounced "cabby."
>
> "He was off a cavi, zoned out."

(See also: Grimmy, Sweet One)

Cent
/sent/
(noun)

A way of describing money, often downplaying a larger amount, and typically referring to sums in a casual or dismissive manner.

> "I know you're not trippin' off that lil five cent ($500) I owe you."

Charlie

/cha-lee/
(adjective)

Having no warrants, nor carrying anything illegal.

> "I ain't trippin' off gettin' blurped by 5-0, I'm Charlie."

Chassy

/chas-ee/
(noun)

A term used to describe a very attractive woman.

> *Believed to originate from the word "chassis," referring to the frame of a vehicle, and used metaphorically to highlight a woman's appealing physical structure.*
>
> "Bruh slid through with a real chassy, had the whole block lookin'."

(See also: Tenda, Top Notch)

Check

/chek/
(verb)

To verbally correct or confront someone who is acting out of line, often with an implied threat to enforce boundaries through consequences. Can also refer to receiving or securing something, usually money, often through hustle or determined effort.

> "He got outta pocket, so I had to check him."

Check Game

/chek gaym/
(phrase)

A directive to pay attention or listen closely to what's being said. Similar in use to "check this out," or "listen up," often signaling important or revealing information.

> "Check game, bruh, I'm finna run down the play."

(See also: Peep Game)

Check Play

/chek play/
(phrase)

An extension of peep game, meaning to pay attention or observe carefully, often to recognize important details or underlying intentions.

> *Most often used immediately after "peep game" in speech, though it can occasionally stand alone.*
>
> "She only come around when you up, bruh. Peep game, check play."

(See also: Check Game, Peep Game)

Chester

/ches-ter/
(noun)

A pejorative term for a pedophile.

> *Originating from the rhyme "Chester the child molester."*
>
> "Bruh seem like a Chester; I don't want him nowhere around me."

Chop

/chop/
(noun)

A large, thick marijuana joint, short for chopper. The name emphasizes size and heaviness compared to a regular joint.

> *"Roll up a chop for the ride."*

Chop Game

/chap gaym/
(verb phrase)

Having a conversation or discussion, often of significance.

> *Refers to "chopping" or dissecting complex issues, unpacking them through knowledge, wisdom, and insight, collectively known as "game."*
>
> *"We was up at the barbershop, just choppin' game."*

(See also: Chop It Up)

Chop It Up

/chop it up/
(verb phrase)

To have a conversation, often one of importance or significance. Closely related to *Chop Game*.

> *Refers to "chopping up" or dissecting a subject through conversation.*
>
> *"I ran into bruh yesterday, and we chopped it up about some real moves."*

(See also: Chop Game)

Chunk 'Em

/chonk um/
(verb phrase)

To fight; often used as a direct challenge or in reference to squaring up with someone.

> "He kept pressin' me, so I told him we could chunk 'em."

(See also: Get Em Up, Go From The Shoulders)

The City

/thuh sit-ee/
(noun)

A common nickname for San Francisco. Often contrasted with The Town (Oakland), highlighting San Francisco's larger, more metropolitan character compared to Oakland's grounded, local identity.

> "We bout to slide to a day party out in The City."

(See also: Frisco, S.F.C., San Fran, The Town)

City Situation

/sit-ee sit-choo-ay-shun/
(phrase)

A term used to describe activities, behaviors, or identity typical of, representing, or associated with San Francisco, California, often referred to as "The City."

> Considered San Francisco's answer to Oakland's "Town Business."
>
> "You already know, it's a City Situation every time we in the building."

(See also: Town Business)

Clean
/kleen/
(adjective)

Describes a nice item, such as a car, clothing, etc., that looks fresh or well-maintained.

> "Damn, when you get that Chevelle? That thang hella clean."

(See also: Raw, Saucy)

Clown
/klown/
(verb)

To put on a performance that draws attention, whether by ridiculing someone and causing embarrassment or by showing out in a bold, demonstrative way.

> Commonly used in the past tense as "clownt."
>
> "She tried to check me, so I clownt her in front of everybody."

(See also: Fronted Off, Put On Blast, Roasted)

Cock
/kok/
(noun)

A mistranslated or misapplied term for female genitalia.

> While the word originally and correctly refers to the male genitalia, in this context it is incorrectly applied exclusively to females.
>
> "He kept talkin' about chasin' cock, but he meant women."

(See also: Pearl)

Coke White
/kohk whyt/
(adjective)

Something that is extremely white in color, drawing a comparison to the color of cocaine.

> "Those new Air Forces are coke white."

Cola
/koh-luh/
(noun)

A term for crack/cocaine.

> Derived from "Coca-Cola."
>
> "He be out there all night servin' straight cola."

(See also: A1 Yola)

Cold Game
/kohld gaym/
(phrase)

Used to describe a situation that's unfair, harsh, or unfortunate, especially when someone is mistreated, unlucky, punished, or caught up in something unethical.

> "They really left bruh hangin', cold game."

Cold Piece Of Work

/kohld piece uh werk/
(phrase)

Said to or about someone whose actions are foul, disloyal, or unreasonable, leaving others disappointed, disbelieving, or appalled.

> "You a cold piece of work for that one, bwoi."

The Coli

/thuh koh-lee/
(noun)

The Oakland Coliseum. Built in 1966 as a multi-purpose stadium, it became a longtime Bay Area landmark. Former home of the Raiders and Athletics.

> Located only a few hundred feet away, Oracle Arena served as the longtime home of the Golden State Warriors from 1971-2019.

> "I remember me and unk went to The Coli to see Marcus Allen back in the day."

Collar Pop

/kah-lah pop/
(noun, verb)

A reference to self-pride or status, whether physical or figurative. Often describes a moment of bold confidence, flair, or symbolic elevation. It expresses behavior that draws attention or showcases confidence, often with an air of superiority or flashiness. Can be literal, as in the physical act of tugging the collar, or figurative, as in verbally bragging.

> "You know I had to pull up and collar pop on em one time."

(See also: Collar Popper, Collar Poppin', Pop Your Collar)

Collar Popper

/kah-lah pop-er/
(noun)

A confident, flashy individual known for standing out; often stylish, smooth, or expressive in how they carry themselves. While typically used with admiration, it can also suggest someone who's doing too much, braggin, or seeking attention.

> "Bruh be putin' it in they face; he a real collar popper."

(See also: Collar Pop, Collar Poppin', Pop Your Collar)

Collar Poppin'

/kah-lah pop-in/
(verb)

A style-driven display of confidence, marked by bold attitude, eye-catching presentation, or the literal gesture of flipping one's collar. Often associated with self-celebration, it can also suggest bragging, showing off, or trying too hard, depending on the tone, setting, or delivery.

> "That new promotion had him collar poppin' all night long."

(See also: Collar Pop, Collar Popper, Pop Your Collar)

Come Thru

/kuhm throo/
(verb phrase)

To arrive or show up in a way that draws attention, often by showcasing something impressive such as a car, outfit, or general presence. Implies confidence, style, or status.

> "I just flipped off the showroom floor, I'm finna come thru."

Come Up

/kum uhp/
(noun)

A situation or opportunity that results in significant gain or profit.

> "They say the only way to come up is to stay down."

Come-A-New

/kuhm-uh-noo/
(verb)

To abandon something old in favor of something better. Often used to describe upgrading, improving, or moving on from something that's inadequate, worn out, or more trouble than it's worth, whether it be a car, outfit, job, or relationship.

> "The check engine light keep comin' on in the mobby, I'm finna have to come-a-new."

(See also: Flip)

Cool On

/kool awn/
(phrase)

Expresses disinterest, rejection, or a change of mind about something, whether an activity, food, person, or idea. Often used in a romantic context.

> Often stylized as "Cool Off."
>
> "I don't like how you been movin'. I'm cool on/off you."

Crankin'

/krayn-kin/
(adjective)

Busy, active, or moving at a steady pace. Often used to describe a party, block, or business that's drawing traffic or handling a lot of volume.

> "Bruh shop stay crankin'; it be a three hour wait on Saturday."

(See also: Movin')

Cream
/kreem/
(noun)

A high-quality mixture of crack cocaine, making it especially desirable.

> "Don't spend down the street, they got straight cream around the corner."

Cross Game
/kraws gaym/
(verb)

The act of breaking spoken or unspoken rules and codes of ethics or loyalty.

> "He tried to cross game and end up gettin' ran off the block."

Cryp
/krip/
(noun)

An extremely potent strain of marijuana, sometimes believed to be laced with another substance.

> Commonly thought to be short for "kryptonite."
>
> A lesser-accepted theory links the name to the Crip gang, drawing on associations with being "laced" and stereotypes around sherm or sherm sticks (joints or cigarettes dipped in PCP or embalming fluid). This interpretation, however, is uncertain and not widely accepted.
>
> "Let's slide through the Red Fence, they got that cryp."

(See also: Bomb, Dank, Gas)

Cuddie

/kuh-dee/
(noun)

A colloquial term similar to bruh, folks, or potna, primarily used in Vallejo and parts of the northern Bay Area to refer to "a trusted ally; someone closer than a friend but with no blood relation."

> *Regional consensus suggests "Cuddie" is the preferred spelling, though "Cutty" and "Cuddy" also appear as alternate forms.*
>
> *The term originates from the Crestside neighborhood of Vallejo and is potentially derived from "cutthoat," a spelling specific to that area, and sometimes thought to blend "cousin" and "buddy." While it may be recognized or used casually in other parts of the Bay, it carries the most cultural weight within its home turf and may not be adopted by individuals from other sections of the same city.*
>
> *"That's my Cuddie from way back, we been solid since kids."*

(See also: Bruh, Folks, Potna, Rogue)

Cupcakin'

/kup-kay-kin/
(verb)

Spending affectionate time with a love interest; being romantic or "soft."

> *"I ain't seen blud in a week. He probably off somewhere cupcakin'."*

Cus Cus

/kuhs-kuhs/
(noun)

A playful or familiar way of saying cousin. Often used among close acquaintances or when referring to someone in the third person. Carries a tone of light humor, affection, or subtle distance depending on delivery.

> "You know Cus Cus always be on some 'ole weird activity."

(See also: Ugly Cuz)

Cut

/kut/
(verb, noun)

A hiding spot or discreet location where someone or something stays out of sight. Also used to refer to the act of leaving or making an exit.

> "That fool was over there layin' in the cut, they ain't even peep him."

(See also: Bounce, Dip, Do It Movin', Shake The Spot, Spin Off, Tucked)

Cuzzo

/kuh-zoh/
(noun)

A friendly term used to address a cousin, close friend, or even a stranger, conveying familiarity and camaraderie. It's often used interchangeably with terms like bro, bruh, or blud.

> "What's good, Cuzzo, you ready for that game tonight, blud?"

(See also: Blud, Bruh, Cuddie, Family, Folks, Loved One, Potna)

"D"
/dee/
(noun)

Short for "dope," typically refers to crack cocaine.

"Back in the day they was ballin' in the D game."

D-Boy
/dee-boy/
(noun)

A drug dealer, most often of crack cocaine.

Debated by some as a misnomer since dope originally referred to heroin, specifically.

"O.G. one of the original old school d-boys."

D-Boy Knot
/dee-boy knot/
(noun)

A large wad of cash, associated with the image of a drug dealer carrying large amounts of money. The phrase reflects both the size of the roll and the cultural association with street hustling.

"He pulled out a D-Boy Knot when it was time to pay."

(See also: Grip)

Damn Near

/dam neer/
(phrase)

Used to affirmatively indicate that something is very close to being true or has almost happened, often implying a strong likelihood or even a definitive yes.

> *"You linked up wit ol' girl last night?" "Damn Near..."*

Dangle

/dang-guhl/
(verb)

To deceive, steal, or get over on someone. Often implies finesse, trickery, or manipulation for personal advantage.

> *The variation "fadangle" is sometimes used for emphasis or stylistic flair.*

> *"Dude ain't to be trusted, he stay tryin' to dangle."*

(See also: Fadangle)

Dangle Roll

/dang-guhl rohl/
(noun)

A trick shot or deliberate manipulation of the dice in a craps game, typically used to gain an unfair advantage.

> *"He hit that dangle roll so smooth, nobody even peeped it."*

(See also: Dangle, Dangler, Fadangle)

Dangler

/dang-ler/
(noun)

A dishonest person, swindler, or thief.

> "Bra was runnin' game the whole time. Straight dangler."

(See also: Dangle, Fadangle)

Dank

/dangk/
(noun)

High-quality, potent marijuana, so named in part for its strong, distinctive odor.

> "He rolled up some dank for the session."

(See also: Indo)

Decent

/DEE-sent/
(adjective)

Used to describe something that is very good, impressive, or attractive. Often applied to food, outfits, or people, with emphasis on the first syllable to signal approval.

> "She walked in lookin' hella thick. I'm like, damn, she decent."

(See also: Clean, Saucy)

Deep

/deep/
(adjective)

Describes the number of people in a group, often implying strength, size, or a formidable presence.

> *"They pulled up nine deep in a van ready to get spunky."*

Deep East

/deep eest/
(noun)

The most eastern section of East Oakland, commonly recognized as the area beyond 73rd Avenue, with Eastmont Mall often cited as a key landmark.

> *Sometimes referred to simply as "The Deep."*
>
> *While there is consensus on the boundary at 73rd Avenue, boundaries extending as far west as Seminary Avenue and High Street are debated.*
>
> *"I tried to tell em The Deep East don't start til you pass Eastmont, but he wanna argue."*

Demo

/dim-moh/
(noun)

Making an example of someone through physical violence, often to prove a point or send a message.

> *Short for "demonstration."*
>
> *"They kept playin' wit him till he laid down the demo."*

Did That
/did that/
(phrase)

An expression of admiration or approval, used to acknowledge that someone executed something exceptionally well. Can follow a compliment or stand alone as praise, with emphasis on did to highlight the excellence or impact of what was done.

> *"That oufit hella cute, girl... you did that."*

Dip
/dip/
(verb)

To leave or depart from a place. Can also refer to a driving technique where the gas and brake pedals are alternated rapidly, causing the car to rock or lift; often done to show off. In another sense, it refers to a man engaging in unprotected sex, likened to "skinny dipping" due to the bare, exposed nature.

> *"We dipped after the function got weird."*
>
> *"He was dippin' on them thangs, front wheel off the ground."*

(See also: Bounce, Cut, Raw Dog, Run Raw, Yikin', Yokin')

Dipped

/dipt/
(adjective, verb)

Dressed in a stylish, coordinated, or impressive manner. Can also refer to being taken down or body-slammed during a fight or altercation.

> "Bruh stayed dipped at every function."

> "He kept bumpin' his gums and got dipped in front of everybody."

Do It Movin'

/doo it moo-vin/
(verb phrase)

To make a move, either physically or metaphorically, especially when leaving a place, avoiding negativity, or progressing in life. Whether stepping away from drama or pushing forward with purpose, it reflects forward momentum.

> "They started actin' funny, so I had to do it movin'."

(See also: Bounce, Cut, Dip, Shake The Spot)

Do The Damn Thang

/doo thuh dam thayng/
(phrase)

An expression meaning to do your thing, proceed confidently with an action, or give encouragement to pursue a goal or task. Can also signal readiness or agreement to move forward with something.

> "It's time to make this play. Let's do the damn thang."

Do The Fool

/doo thuh fool/
(verb phrase)

To act out in an extreme, disruptive, or over-the-top manner, whether from anger, frustration, or for attention. Can refer to escalating conflict, causing a scene, or doing something dramatically outside the norm.

> "Soon as the drank kicked in, he got to doin the fool."

(See also: Trippin')

Do Ya Thug Thang

/doo yuh thug thayng/
(phrase)

An expression meaning to do your thing, handle your business, or confidently pursue your goals or actions, often with a street-oriented or bold undertone.

> *Often phrased as "do ya thug thizzle."*
>
> "I see you movin', bruh. Go 'head and do ya thug thang."

Doin' Bad

/doo-in bad/
(verb phrase)

In a state of physical or financial hardship. Commonly used to describe someone who is broke, unhoused, unclean, or visibly declining in well-being. May also apply to drug addiction or long-term struggle.

> "Bruh used to be a factor, but now he out here doin' bad."

(See also: Hurt)

Doin' It Big

/doin it big/
(phrase)

Doing something at a high level of scale or quality, often in a celebratory way or with little to no restraint. Refers to moments, events, or activities where indulgence, excess, and abundance are central to the experience.

> "It must've been 'bout 20 crabs in that gumbo, we did it big."

Doin' The Most

/doo-in thuh mohst/
(phrase)

Engaging in exaggerated, demonstrative, or unnecessarily dramatic behavior, often for attention or effect. Can also refer to going overboard in a way that draws criticism, especially when someone is being excessively demonstrative beyond what the situation calls for.

> "Bruh was doin' the most at the function, actin' like it was his birthday."

(See also: Doin' Too Much, Extra, Extra'd Out)

Doin' Too Much

/doo-in too much/
(verb phrase)

Engaging in behavior that is exaggerated, inauthentic, or unnecessary. Often refers to trying too hard, pretending to impress others, or going farther than the situation requires.

> *"Be cool wit all that extra flexin' bra, you doin' too much."*

(See also: 4 Much, Doin' The Most, Extra, Extra'd Out)

Doja

/doh-juh/
(noun)

A type of high-quality marijuana.

> *Likely derived from "Indonesian," similar to indo.*
>
> *Popularized through West Coast rap culture in the 1990s.*
>
> *"Cuzzo slid thru wit a fat sack of that doja."*

(See also: Dank, Indo)

Dolla

/dah-luh/
(noun)

A Bay Area pronunciation of dollar, used to mean one hundred dollars rather than a single dollar.

> Commonly used when referring to amounts in hundreds, where two dollas means $200, three dollas means $300, and so on.
>
> "I paid three dollas for them kicks, but they was worth it."

(See also: Cent, Hunnid)

Donut

/doh-nuht/
(noun)

A car maneuver that involves driving or drifting in a tight circle at high speed, often performed as a show of driving skill or for entertainment.

> This technique was popularized by Oakland, CA sideshows in the 1980s and 1990s.
>
> "He bent the block on Hegenberger and swung a donut, right in front of 5-0."

(See also: Swang)

Dope Fiend

/dope feend/
(noun)

A crack cocaine / drug addict.

> *Regarded by some as a misnomer (similar to "D-Boy"), as the term "dope" was at one time applied almost exclusively to heroin.*
>
> *"She used to be hella fine, now she a cold dope fiend."*

Dope Fiends

/dope feenz/
(noun)

Slang for matches used for smoking when a lighter is unavailable. Can also refer to the plural of dope fiend, describing individuals addicted to drugs.

> *"I ain't got no lighter; I think I got some dope fiends in the car."*

Dosin'

/doh-sin/
(verb)

Performing high-performance car maneuvers, such as donuts or figure eights, often to show off or for entertainment.

> *"He was at the sideshow last night, dosin' that thang."*

(See also: Servin')

Double Up

/dub-uhl uhp/
(noun)

A wholesale quantity of cocaine, typically crack, priced and portioned with the expectation that the buyer can double their investment by selling it retail.

> "I went and copped me a double up and flipped it in 2 hours."

(See also: Bubble, Plug)

Dougie

/dug-ee/
(noun)

A personal style, approach, or way of carrying yourself. Refers to someone's unique flair, demeanor, or confidence.

> "Oh, that's how you movin'? It's all good; do your dougie."

Downt

/down-t/
(verb)

A pronunciation of downed, meaning murdered or killed, usually in reference to gun violence. Used to describe someone being taken out or fatally struck.

> "They downt him outside the liquor store."

(See also: Knocked Down, Laminated, Smacked, Smoked)

Drank

/drangk/
(noun)

An alcoholic beverage, often a mixture containing hard liquor.

> *Not to be confused with the Houston/Southern term for promethazine-codeine syrup (lean), popularized by DJ Screw and chopped-and-screwed culture.*
>
> "You loaded? You smell like hella drank."

Drop

/drahp/
(noun)

Short for "droptop," a convertible car.

> "He got the drop 'Stang on thangs, given' em the business."

Dry Run

/dry ruhn/
(noun)

An unproductive effort or trip that fails to achieve its intended purpose, resulting in a waste of time or effort.

> "We slid all the way to Sac about that play, but it was a dry run."

Dry Snitch

/dry snich/
(verb, noun)

To indirectly snitch, usually by hinting, implying, or revealing information without openly admitting it. Almost always intentional, done to expose someone while pretending not to. Can also refer to an individual who engages in this behavior.

> "Talkin' bout who did what in front of the boss, that's dry snitchin'."

(See also: Tellin')

Dub

/duhb/
(noun)

The number 20 in any context. Can also refer to the letter W, most often used as a nickname for someone whose last name, and sometimes first name, starts with W.

> "Blud, let me hold dub right quick."
>
> "You know Kevin Williams? That's K-Dub."

(See also: Twomp)

Ducked Off

/duhkt awf/
(adjective)

That which is in a secluded location, hidden.

> By extension, a secluded or little-known space may be referred to as a "duck off" (noun).
>
> "I'm just chillin'. Ducked off out the way at this lil unda spot."

(See also: Tucked, Under)

Dumb

/dum/
(adjective)

Used to describe something as extreme, excessive, or to an intense degree. Depending on context, it can express strong approval or criticism.

> "That new slap go dumb hard."
>
> "She was talkin' dumb reckless."

(See also: Go Crazy, Go Dumb, Go Stupid, Hella)

Dumb-ass

/dum-ass/
(adverb)

A slang intensifier similar to "hella," used to emphasize a very high degree of something, similar to "extra" or "a lot."

> "On my momma, I'm dumb-ass hungry."

(See also: Hella)

Dummy

/dum-ee/
(adjective)

Describes something or someone as extreme, excessive, or highly impressive, often emphasizing energy, excitement, or impact beyond expectations. Can also refer to acting with unrestrained energy or uninhibited expression, whether physical, emotional, confrontational, or performative.

> "The function went dummy last night."
>
> "That chain dummy."

(See also: Dumb, Go, Go Crazy, Go Dumb, Go Stupid, Hyphy)

Dusted & Disgusted

/dus-tid an dis-cus-tid/
(adjective)

A phrase describing someone who's struggling financially or going through hard times; often used to convey being broke, depleted, or generally doing poorly. Can also refer to a period when things aren't going right, when both resources and morale are low, implying both financial and emotional frustration.

> *Originally derived from the 1995 E-40 song "Dusted 'n' Disgusted," the phrase has evolved from its initial depiction of betrayal and street frustration to express a broader sense of financial hardship or life struggle, often detached from the song's original meaning.*
>
> "Rent due, the whip in the shop, I'm dusted & disgusted right now."

(See also: Doin' Bad, Financially Embarrassed, Off, Pockets Touchin')

E-1-4

/ee-wun-foe/
(noun)

International Boulevard, formerly known as East 14th Street, in Oakland, CA. The abbreviation "E-1-4" reflects the street's original name and its enduring local significance.

> *"It was hella traffic on 880 so I just rode E-1-4 all the way to the hut."*

E-mac

/ee-mak/
(noun)

An abbreviated form of immaculate, used to describe something exceptionally clean, stylish, or well-put-together. Often refers to appearance, performance, or presentation.

> *"Bruh restored the old school from the frame, got that thang lookin' E-mac."*

(See also: Clean, Saucy)

E.P.A.

/ee-pee-ay/
(initialism, noun)

The commonly used initialism for "East Palo Alto", California; the preferred regional term.

> *"I got a lil top-notch in E.P.A. I'm finna hook up wit later on."*

(See also: E.S.O., S.F.C.)

E.S.O.
/ee-ess-oh/
(initialism, noun)

Initialism for Eastside Oakland. A geographic identifier and cultural marker representing the neighborhoods and communities on Oakland's east side. Often used with pride to signify local identity, upbringing, or affiliation.

> *"Some fool was in the bathroom taggin' E.S.O. on every stall."*

(See also: Deep East, E.P.A., S.F.C., The Town)

Ear Hustle
/eer hust-l/
(verb)

To Eavesdrop, overhear, or listen in on conversations.

> *"She act like she wasn't listenin', but she was tryna ear hustle the whole time."*

Elroy
/el-roy/
(noun)

A play on the letter L, used in different contexts. Commonly refers to a life sentence in prison (L), or in plural form (elroys), to a driver's license (L's).

> *"Bruh caught an Elroy on that case."*

> *"I gotta renew my elroys before the end of the month."*

(See also: All Day, Kickstand, L's, Washed)

Errythang

/air-ee-thang/
(adverb)

A colloquial expression for "everything."

> "Bet I knock me a new breezy tonight, I'm on errythang movin'."

Extra

/ek-struh/
(adjective)

Describes behavior that is overly dramatic or excessive, such as being unnecessarily loud or overreacting. Sometimes used more broadly to describe anything extreme or over-the-top, similar to hella.

> "She was bein' hella extra off the alcohol."

(See also: Doin' The Most, Extra'd Out, Hella)

Extra'd Out

/ek-struhd owt/
(adjective)

Exhibiting behavior or qualities that are excessively dramatic or over-the-top, aligned with being "extra."

> "You feelin' yourself tonight, huh? You extra'd out."

(See also: Extra)

F*** Wit Me

/f*** wit mee/
(verb phrase)

A request for support, trust, or inclusion. Can mean inviting someone to join in, asking for a chance, or seeking acknowledgment and involvement. Often said with the expectation of mutual respect, loyalty, or understanding.

"I got a play up that's about to go silly. You might wanna f*** wit me on this one."

F****n' Around

/f***-in uh-rownd/
(verb phrase)

Doing nothing in particular. Often refers to spending time without a specific purpose, going with the flow, or loosely participating in whatever is happening. Similar in tone to hanging out or casually checking in on what's going on.

"I ain't really on nothin', just f****n' around for a minute."

(See also: Kick It)

F****n' Em

/f***-in um/
(verb phrase)

Short for "f****n' em up." Used to describe someone doing exceptionally well, standing out, or making a strong impression, usually in terms of style, success, or presence.

> "He slid through in that coke white drop with the top down. Bruh f****n' em."

F****n' Wit It

/f***-in wit it/
(verb phrase)

Participating in or going along with something, often to a high degree. Used to acknowledge when someone is deeply engaged, excelling, or showing focus and skill.

> "They been rockin' every day for the last 2 months. They f****n' wit it tuff."

Faasst

/fah-yst/
(exclamation)

Indicates immediacy or total agreement.

> "Let's go get to the money, bra." "Faasst!"

(See also: Fasho, Off Top)

Factor

/fak-ter/
(noun)

A relevant or influential member of the community whose presence or actions carry significant weight. Can also refer to a person with power, money, and influence in the drug trade, often dealing in large quantities or occupying a high position in the hierarchy.

> *Commonly preceded by "major," as in "major factor."*
>
> *"Bruh been a factor in The Town for years."*

(See also: Major Factor)

Fadangle

/fuh-dang-guhl/
(verb)

To deceive, cheat, or gain an advantage through dishonest means. Often used to describe getting over on someone by manipulation or unfair dealing.

> *"Bruh tried to fadangle his way out of paying."*

(See also: Dangle, Dangle Roll, Dangler)

Fadin'

/fay-din/
(verb)

Engaging with someone romantically or sexually, often casually or non-exclusively. Often suggests an ongoing or recurring dynamic, rather than a one-time encounter.

> *"He still trippin' off this lil chick we was both fadin' back in the day."*

Fag Off

/fag awf/
(phrase)

To leave a relationship for a selfish or unwarranted reason, typically used in reference to a woman, often suggesting behavior akin to that of a prostitute's abrupt departure.

> † This term is not related to and should not be confused with any derogatory or pejorative terms used to describe sexual orientation.
>
> "She fagged off, but don't change the locks, she'll be back."

(See also: Blow Up)

Faggit

/fag-it/
(noun)

A derogatory term used to describe a woman characterized by traits such as selfishness, rudeness, dishonesty, or lack of accountability, in varying combinations.

> † This term is not related to and should not be confused with any derogatory or pejorative terms used to describe sexual orientation.
>
> "She always tryna use his kids against him, straight faggit."

(See also: Punk Rock)

Fake

/fayk/
(verb)

Fail to show up or follow through, often at the last minute.

> "Don't forget you supposed to help me move, and you bet not fake."

Fake Feelin' It

/fayk feel-in it/
(verb phrase)

Pretending to be excited, confident, or enjoying yourself, especially in social settings.

> *"She actin' like she havin' fun, but you can tell she fake feelin' it."*

(See also: Perpetrate)

Fake Kick It

/fayk kick-it/
(verb phrase)

To pretend to enjoy a social situation, gathering, or interaction while actually feeling bored, uncomfortable, or uninterested. The term highlights a lack of genuine connection or enjoyment, often implying someone is only present out of obligation or appearances.

> *"I ain't much care for baby attitude, and I wasn't bout to fake kick it."*

(See also: Fake Feelin' It, Perpetrate)

Fake Nutty

/fayk nuh-tee/
(verb phrase)

To pretend to have an emotional outburst or act erratically as a tactic. Often used to gain sympathy, avoid accountability, deflect from a situation, or draw attention away from the real issue.

> Likely a successor to the earlier expression "playin' the nut role," a term associated with pimp culture.
>
> "Soon as they started askin' questions, she tried to pull a fake nutty."

(See also: Nutty)

Fakeway

/fayk-way/
(adverb)

Somewhat or to a certain extent.

> "He be out here tryna fake way tryna stunt tho."

(See also: Lightweight)

Fam-Bam

/fam-bam/
(noun)

A playful and affectionate term for family.

> "Our mommas grew up together, that's my fam-bam."

Family

/fam-uh-lee/
(noun)

A term of address used to greet or refer to someone in a familiar, affectionate, or respectful way, similar to "bro" or "homie," and commonly used among close friends or trusted associates.

> "What's up, Family? What you on today?"

Fasheezy

/fuh-shee-zee/
(adverb)

A playful or exaggerated variation of "for sure," originating in Oakland, popularized in Bay Area slang.

> "The function was off the heezy fasheezy."

(See also: Fasho, Fasholy)

Fasho

/fuh-shoh/
(adverb)

A variation of "for sure," used to express agreement or confirmation.

> "We fasho gon' link up, soon as I touchdown."

(See also: Fasheezy, Fasholy)

Fasholy

/fuh-show-lee/
(adverb)

A stylized variation of "for surely," used to express agreement, confirmation, or emphasis. An amplified version of Fasho.

> "I appreciate the love bra, fasholy."

(See also: Fasheezy, Fasho)

Faulty

/fawl-tee/
(adjective)

Describes a person or situation lacking reliability, integrity, or fairness. Often used to call out betrayal, dishonesty, or poor character.

> "I ain't really rockin' wit bruh right now; he been movin' kinda faulty."

Federal

/fed-er-uhl/
(adjective)

A manner or style that is notably respectable, implying a polished and sophisticated demeanor. It conveys a sense of elevation and superiority, often associated with a refined or advanced level of presentation.

> "Roll up that window, bruh, we ridin' federal."

Feelin' Me Fingers

/fee-lin mee fing-gerz/
(phrase)

A style of handshake where two parties touch and wiggle fingers, often saying "You feel me?"

> *"Everytime he make a point he get to doin' the feelin' me fingers."*

(See also: No Fingerprints)

Feelin' Myself

/fee-lin my-self/
(verb phrase)

Feeling extremely confident or good about oneself.

> *"I just got my hair done, I'm feelin' myself."*

(See also: Feelin' Yourself)

Feelin' Yourself

/fee-lin yo-self/
(verb phrase)

Typically said in response to someone who is in rare form, clearly in high spirits, unusually confident, animated, or showing out. Can be playful or sarcastic, depending on the moment. Sometimes used to acknowledge someone doing well or enjoying their shine; other times, it's a light check on behavior that feels extra, performative, or out of character.

> *"Oh wow, you really feelin' yourself tonight, huh?"*

(See also: Doin' Too Much, Extra'd Out, Feelin' Myself)

Fetti

/fet-ee/
(noun)

Money; cash. Commonly used to refer to wealth or currency in general.

> *Sometimes pronounced "feddi."*
>
> *The term fetti is thought by some to be a shortening of federal (as in U.S. federal reserve notes). Others have noted its similarity in both sound and meaning to the Spanish slang "feria" (money), a term commonly used in California. Some have also speculated that it may be a clipping of confetti, small pieces of paper thrown in celebration, possibly in allusion to money falling. Though unproven, these connections may have influenced the word's development and popularity.*
>
> *"I'm tryna stack this fetti and stay out the way."*

(See also: Bank, Paper, Skrilla)

Fifty

/fif-tee/
(noun)

A Ford Mustang 5.0, referencing the 5.0-liter engine. Commonly used to describe both the engine and the car itself, especially models popular in street culture.

> *Sometimes phonetically altered and playfully pronounced "nifty."*
>
> *"Bruh just pulled up in a clean fifty."*

Financially Embarrassed

/fye-nan-shuh-lee em-bair-uhst/
(adjective)

Lacking funds; temporarily broke or in a financially strained position. Often said jokingly or sarcastically to soften the blow of admitting you're low on money.

> "I ain't broke, I'm just financially embarrassed right now."

(See also: Off, Pockets Touchin')

Finna

/fin-nuh/
(contraction)

About to do something; preparing to act. Commonly used to express immediate intent or a plan to take action.

> Derived from "fixin' to."
>
> Sometimes stylized as "finsta."
>
> "I'm finna quit my job and start my own business."

Fired On

/fiyrd awn/
(verb phrase)

To be struck with a sudden punch, often without warning.

> "First person even look at me wrong gettin' fired on."

(See also: Bank, Stole On, Take Off)

Fit

/fit/
(noun)

Short for outfit, typically implying a coordinated, stylish, or well-put-together look.

> *"Bruh came through with a clean fit at the function."*

Fitted

/fit-tid/
(adjective)

Being well-dressed; in a stylish and coordinated outfit. Refers to a person's overall clothing and style combination.

> *"Everytime I see him he saucy. On mommas, bruh stay fitted."*

(See also: Lavishly Coordinated)

Five Finger Discount

/fyv fing-er dis-cownt/
(noun)

A term for stealing or shoplifting; refers to acquiring something without paying for it.

> *"He came up on a five finger discount at the mall."*

(See also: For The "F")

Flash
/flash/
(verb)

To have a sudden outburst of anger, usually directed at someone who caused offense or disrespect. Often triggered when a person feels fed up, tested, or pushed past their limit.

> "Bruh tried to test me, so I flashed on him."

(See also: Nut Up, Nutty, On One)

The Flatlands
/thuh flat-landz/
(noun)

The section of Deep East Oakland that includes and extends below MacArthur Boulevard, characterized by its relatively level terrain compared to the hillier regions of the city.

> *Sometimes shortened or abbreviated as "the Flats."*

> "He stay in Grass Valley, but his girl from the Flats."

Flight To Boston
/flyt to baw-stin/
(phrase)

A coded reference to fellatio, playing off the "bos" sound in "Boston" and its link to the slang "boss."

> *Sometimes extended with "on the red-eye," as a playful hint at the aftermath.*

> "She gave him a flight to Boston after the function... on the red-eye."

(See also: Boss)

Flip

/flip/
(verb)

To buy or purchase something, often used casually to describe acquiring big-ticket items like cars, jewelry, or property.

> *"Cuzzo just flipped a Benz."*

(See also: Snatch)

Flossin'

/flaw-sin/
(verb)

To show off and enjoy one's success or possessions, typically in public and through material things like cars, clothes, or jewelry, in a way that draws attention. Often done with style and confidence, it reflects pride and self-celebration, though it can also carry a subtle critique when seen as excessive.

> *"He slid through the picnic in the drop-top, just flossin', gettin' hella love."*

(See also: Highside)

Fluke

/flook/
(noun)

An unexpected or random occurrence, either positive or negative, often happening by chance without planning.

> *"I ran into her again the very next day on a straight fluke."*

Fluker

/floo-ker/
(noun)

A promiscuous woman, often dated out of boredom or convenience.

> "Call them lil flukers from last night."

Folded

/fohl-did/
(adjective)

Knocked out or incapacitated from a punch.

> "Bruh kept runnin' his mouth and got folded."

Folks

/fohks/
(noun)

A friend or close associate; also used in the context of a relationship between a prostitute and pimp.

> "That's been my folks since back in the day."

(See also: Cuddie, Fam-Bam, Potna, Rogue)

Fool

/fool/
(noun)

A familiar expression that usually connotes admiration, boldness, or talent, though sometimes recklessness. It can also serve casually in conversation as a way of referring to someone. Most often, it carries a positive tone, highlighting daring, humor, or skill.

> *The final L is frequently softened in pronunciation and may appear written or spoken as *foo.*
>
> "What's up, fool, what you up to?"
>
> "Nephew could dance his ass off, I'm tellin' you, he a straight fool wit it."

Foot'n It

/foot-n it/
(verb phrase)

Traveling by foot, typically due to a lack of transportation. Often used derogatorily to highlight someone's immobility or absence of a vehicle.

> "He ain't never had a car, he be foot'n it everywhere."

For The "F"

/fa da ef/
(phrase)

For free; used to emphasize that something cost nothing or was given without charge.

> "She slid me the plate for the F."

Fresh Out

/fresh owt/
(phrase)

Recently released from jail or prison, often used to mark someone's return to everyday life after doing time.

> Sometimes also phrased as "fresh home."
>
> "Bruh fresh out and already back on his grind."

Frisco

/fris-koh/
(noun)

Another name for San Francisco. The preferred term among locals, as opposed to San Fran, a term rarely, if ever, used by native residents.

> Using "San Fran" is often seen as a clear sign of being a non-native resident, visitor, or transplant.
>
> "Bruh got folks out in Frisco we can tap in with."

(See also: The City, S.F.C., San Fran)

Front Street

/fruhnt street/
(noun)

A figurative way of saying someone has been exposed or put in the spotlight, usually in an embarrassing or vulnerable way.

> "Don't put my business on Front Street like that."

(See also: Fronted Off, Put On Blast)

Fronted Off
/fruhnt-ed off/
(verb phrase)

To be exposed or embarrassed in front of others, often as a result of someone revealing something personal or putting you on the spot.

> "Bruh fronted me off in front of everybody."

(See also: Clown, Front Street, Put On Blast)

Function
/fuhnk-shin/
(noun)

A party or social gathering. Also used to describe socializing or participating in the activity.

> "The function gon be movin' tonight."
>
> "I'm up in this g-thang tryin' to function one time."

Funk
/fonk/
(noun)

Conflict, beef, or trouble; a tense or volatile situation.

> Often pronounced "fonk" in usage.
>
> "The funk is on."

(See also: The Funk Is On)

The Funk Is On

/thuh fonk iz awn/
(phrase)

A declaration of war or high-level conflict; often a direct statement that conflict is escalating.

> "Funk" is often pronounced "fonk" in usage.
>
> "The funk been on since they downt lil cuz."

(See also: Funk)

Funny Style

/fun-ee styl/
(adjective phrase)

Overly cautious, stingy, or controlling, especially concerning personal belongings or money. Despite the wording, it does not mean that someone's style is humorous; rather, it implies guarded or possessive behavior.

> "Bruh actin' funny style about his ride, like we gon' scratch it or somethin'."

G-Thang

/gee thayng/
(noun)

A versatile placeholder term used to highlight or emphasize whatever is central to the situation, whether an event, object, or activity. Its meaning shifts with context, but it carries a stronger sense of weight or flair than simply saying *that thang.

> "The function was lit, we was up in that G-Thang."

G.O.D.

/gee-oh-dee/
(phrase)

A forceful way to affirm the truth or seriousness of a statement, often used at the end of a sentence for emphasis.

> "She had the whole block shut down, G.O.D."

(See also: On God, On Mommas)

GAME

In the Bay Area, game isn't just a word, it's a way of life. Born from street wisdom, sharpened through social dynamics, and passed down like oral scripture, game is the lens through which people move, hustle, and connect. It refers to knowledge, strategy, influence, and style, not just what you know, but how you use it. Not just what you do, but how you do it.

In the Bay Area, game is a religion.

The 1973 film The Mack, shot in and based on Oakland, remains one of the most iconic cinematic representations of this principle, delivering more raw game per frame than perhaps any movie before or since. Even Tupac Shakur, born in New York and raised across several cities, claimed Oakland as the place that shaped him. "Oakland is where I learned the game," he once said. And in return, the Town has long embraced him as one of its own, memorializing him with a street bearing his name.

While The Mack helped define game's association with style, speech, and the pimp archetype, the Bay has also shaped game into something far deeper. Here, game moves strategically; on intellectual, political, and economic levels. You see it in the revolutionary work of the Black Panther Party, in the independent grind of Too Short and E-40, and in the grassroots "out the trunk" mentality that turned hustle into heritage. Both street-smart and self-taught, the Bay has long made game look like entrepreneurship, activism, and empowerment.

In the Bay, you don't have to be in the streets to have game, because game is less about street credentials and more about your approach, your energy, and how you move. Whether someone is gamed up, spittin' game, or asked to peep game, the term speaks to an ability to navigate the world with finesse, understanding, and control. It's a blueprint, a mindset, and in many ways, the foundation of the language itself.

Game

/gaym/
(noun)

A blend of knowledge, wisdom, and strategic understanding, often displayed through actions or speech with a persuasive or charismatic edge. It refers to valuable, practical information and the ability to navigate situations, people, and opportunities effectively. While some associate game with manipulation or deception, in its essence, game is about clarity, discernment, awareness, and alignment with the truth.

> "He got too much game to let them play him."

(See also: Mouthpiece)

The Game

/thuh gaym/
(noun)

A term that refers broadly to street life and the system of rules, codes, and conduct that govern it. Often short for "the dope game" or "pimp game," but used more generally to describe the world of the criminal hustle. It includes not just the activities themselves, but also the mindset, values, and expectations that define participation.

> "I had a lil setback, but I ain't trippin'. That's a part of the game."

Game Goofy

/gaym-goo-fee/
(adjective)

Lacking awareness, understanding, or application of game; especially in social, romantic, or street-related situations. Describes someone who is blind to social cues, street dynamics, or the unspoken rules of interaction. Often marked by poor situational awareness, naivety, and an inability to navigate moments that require tact, confidence, or street smarts.

> "Bruh tried to holler at both of 'em at the same time; hella game goofy."

Game Laced

/gaym layss't/
(phrase)

Having been thoroughly educated or equipped with valuable knowledge, wisdom, or strategic insight.

> "He came up under real ones, so you know he game laced."

(See also: Game, Game Tight, Gamed Up)

Game Recognize Game

/gaym-reck-uh-nize-gaym/
(phrase)

A saying that means skilled, knowledgeable, or experienced individuals can identify and acknowledge the same qualities in others. Often used to show mutual respect or understanding between people with similar expertise or street smarts.

> "When bruh walked in, I already knew what he was about. Game recognize game."

Game Related

/gaym ruh-lay-tid/
(adjective)

Connected to or reflecting game; describing actions, speech, or knowledge that demonstrate wisdom, strategy, clarity, and the ability to navigate situations or influence others effectively.

> "Bruh don't speak on nothin' unless it's game related."

(See also: Game, Player)

Game Tight

/gaym-tyte/
(adjective)

Possessing a high level of knowledge, awareness, skill, wisdom, or strategy. Refers to someone whose game is strong, complete, consistent, well-developed, and impenetrable, making their approach polished, reliable, and difficult to challenge or manipulate.

> *"Bruh game tight, he always know how to move."*

(See also: Game, Game Laced, Game Related, Gamed Up, Player)

Gamed Up

/gaymd-up/
(adjective)

Someone who has been taught, has acquired, or is in possession of valuable information. Describes a person who is well-informed, knowledgeable, and prepared, especially in matters requiring strategy, awareness, or social skill.

> *"Lil bruh gamed up, he know how to move in any crowd."*

(See also: Game, Game Laced, Game Related, Game Tight)

Gas

/gass/
(noun, verb, adjective)

A versatile term used to describe something of exceptional quality, especially high-grade marijuana, entertaining rap lyrics, or anything intensely enjoyable or impressive. Can be used as a noun, verb, or adjective depending on context.

> "This plate is gas, I might need seconds."
>
> "You heard bra go in on that beat? He was gasin'."

(See also: Bomb, Good)

Geekin'

/gee-kin/
(verb)

Behaving strangely, usually under the influence of drugs.

> "You good bra? You over there geekin'."

(See also: Gurpin', Tweakin')

Geesin'

/gee-sin/
(verb)

Acting irrationally, overly emotional, or strangely. Overreacting or behaving in a way that seems excessive or unreasonable to others.

> *Comparable to New York's "buggin'."*
>
> "Chill out, bruh, you lightweight geesin'."

(See also: Trippin')

Get Active

/git-ak-tiv/
(verb phrase)

To take action, often in pursuit of financial gain or in preparation for violence.

> *"We done kicked back long enough, breh, it's 'bout time to get active."*

(See also: Bout That Action)

Get At

/git-at/
(verb)

To talk to someone in a flirtatious or direct way.

> *"Remember lil mama from Berkeley? I tried to get at her last night."*

(See also: Holla, Pop)

Get Back

/git-bak/
(verb phrase)

To regain success, recover, or reassert oneself after a loss, setback, or act of disrespect. Can refer to rebounding socially, financially, or personally, as well as retaliating to restore balance or settle a score.

> *"I'm doin' bad right now; I need to get some get back."*

(See also: Brought Back)

Get Down

/gidown/
(noun)

A person's behavior, habits, or lifestyle, often referring to their typical actions or preferences.

> "That's all you wit the cocaine; that ain't even my get down."

(See also: Dougie, Rockin')

Get Em Up

/git-um-up/
(verb phrase)

To engage directly in a confrontation, typically physical, but also used more broadly to describe any face-to-face challenge or conflict.

> "Let's get 'em up then, since you feel some type of way."

(See also: Chunk 'Em, Go From The Shoulders)

Get It

/git-it/
(verb)

To earn or accumulate wealth, success, or status; can also express readiness, encouragement, or determination to take action, similar to saying "let's do it."

> "She out here grindin' every day to get it."
>
> "Aight then, let's get it!"

Get Little
/git-lih-dul/
(verb phrase)

To leave quickly or evade a situation, often to avoid attention or confrontation. The expression suggests slipping away, becoming less visible, or disappearing from view, and is associated with the idea of "ducking down" to remain unnoticed.

> "When the police rolled up, I had to get little."
> "She started trippin', so I got little on her."

Get Off Where You Mad At
/git awf wair yoo mad at/
(phrase)

A challenge or suggestion for someone to physically act on their anger if it has escalated to a serious level. Often used to provoke a fight or tell someone to confront or resolve the issue physically rather than just talk about it.

> "If you feel some type of way, get off where you mad at."

Get On
/git awn/
(verb)

To directly engage someone, whether through confrontation or pursuit. Can refer to attacking someone physically, or approaching someone romantically or flirtatiously, depending on context.

> "They caught him at the stoplight and got on him."
>
> "Damn, she look hella good, get on her, bro."

(See also: Get At, Holla)

Get Wit Your Program
/git wit yo pro-gram/
(verb phrase)

To violently engage someone, often as a form of correction or disciplinary action.

> *The word program is sometimes shortened to "PG," as in "get wit your PG."*
>
> "If he don't come up wit that money, they gon get wit his program."

Get Your Money On
/git-chuh mun-ee awn/
(verb phrase)

To pursue or possess significant financial success. Can refer to the act of making money or the state of already having it.

> *In some contexts, also phrased as "got my money on" to indicate already having money or doing well financially.*
>
> "Ain't no hate over here, bruh. Get your money on."

Gettin' It

/git-in it/
(verb phrase)

Actively earning or accumulating money, often implying success and financial prosperity; making money; Hustling.

> "She got two jobs and a hustle. She out here gettin' it."

(See also: Banked Up, Caked Up, Get Your Money On, Havin' It)

Ghostride

/gohst-ryd/
(verb)

To exit a moving vehicle and dance, perform, or walk beside it while it continues rolling, usually at a slow speed.

> "Bruh hopped out the whip and got to ghostridin' that thang."

(See also: The Hyphy Movement)

Giggin'

/gig-in/
(verb)

Dancing with energy and enthusiasm, often with a distinct Bay Area style or attitude.

> "They had the whole function giggin' to that old-school slap."

(See also: Hittin' It)

Givin' Up Game
/giv-in up gaym/
(verb phrase)

To divulge sensitive or private information, often in ways that break trust. Can refer to snitching, pillow talking, gossiping, or otherwise revealing something meant to be kept quiet. The phrase carries a negative connotation, suggesting a breach of loyalty, discretion, or common sense.

> "You can't tell bruh nathaniel, he be out here givin' up game."

(See also: Breathin')

Go
/goh/
(verb)

Used to describe something that's exceptionally good, exciting, or intense.

> Often a shortened form of phrases like "go dumb," "go stupid," or "go crazy."

> "This beat go."

> "That fit go, bruh."

(See also: Go Crazy, Go Dumb, Go Stupid)

Go Crazy

/go cray-zee/
(verb phrase)

To describe something exceptionally good, impressive, or exciting; often used to praise music, performance, style, or food.

> Commonly phrased as "goin' crazy" in casual speech.
>
> "This beat goin' crazy."
>
> "Man, these tacos go crazy."

(See also: Go, Go Dumb, Go Stupid)

Go Dumb

/goh dum/
(verb phrase)

To dance, act, or react with outrageous, unrestrained energy or intensity, often in response to music, provocation, or excitement.

> "Keep playin' wit me, I'ma go dumb on you."
>
> "This beat go dumb."

(See also: Go, Go Crazy, Go Stupid, Hyphy)

Go From The Shoulders

/goh frum tha show-duhz/
(phrase)

To settle a conflict with a fist fight, without the use of weapons. Usually phrased as a challenge, as in "Let's go from the shoulders."

> Sometimes shortened in casual reference to "from the shoulders."
>
> "Put the gun down and let's go from the shoulders."

(See also: Chunk 'Em, Get Em Up)

Go Out

/go-owt/
(verb phrase)

To compromise your values, self-respect, or dignity, especially in a way that shows weakness, submission, or a lack of integrity. May involve accepting poor treatment or backing down in a cowardly way. Also expressed as Sellin' or Sellin' Out, these phrases are often used as a critique ("You went out," "You sellin'"), or as a warning or suggestion to maintain composure and pride ("Don't go out").

> *"She was talkin' wild and you ain't say nothin'? You went out, bruh."*
>
> *"You over there beggin' for her number, don't go out, blood."*

(See also: Sellin')

Go Stupid

/goh stoo-pid/
(verb phrase)

To act with extreme energy or intensity, often in response to music, emotion, or the surrounding environment. Can refer to dancing, performing at a high level, or reacting in a sudden, aggressive way.

> *"This beat go stupid."*

(See also: Go, Go Crazy, Go Dumb)

Gold Ones
/gold wunz/
(noun)

A name for gold-plated wire-spoke wheels.

> *Interchangeable with "Thangs" or "Gold Thangs."*
>
> *"He pulled up clean, sittin' on gold ones."*

(See also: Gold Thangs, Thangs)

Gold Thangs
/gold thayngz/
(noun)

Gold-plated wire-spoke wheels, often made by Zenith or Dayton and seen on customized old schools. A staple of Bay Area car culture, associated with pride, success, and status.

> *Also referred to as "Thangs" or "Gold Ones."*
>
> *"I just slapped some gold thangs on the old school."*

(See also: Gold Ones, Thangs)

Good
/good/
(noun)

A term used to refer to marijuana, typically implying a high quality, or potent strain.

> *"I'm 'bout to twist some of this good and kick back."*

(See also: Bomb, Gas)

Good Lookin'

/good look-in/
(noun)

A casual expression of thanks or appreciation.

> "Good lookin', bruh. I owe you one."

Got Me Bent

/got me bent/
(phrase)

Used to express that someone is doing or saying something disrespectful or out of line, often suggesting they are testing or misunderstanding personal boundaries or values.

> "You talkin' reckless like I ain't gon say nothin'; you got me bent, blud."

Government

/guhv-uh-mint/
(noun)

Your full (government) name.

> "Bruh over there bumpin' em for real. Gave 'em my whole government and errythang."

Grandaddy

/gran-da-dee/
(noun)

A potent strain of marijuana, often recognized for its strength and heavy effects.

> *"Bruh pulled up wit that Grandaddy, had everybody on stuck."*

Grapes

/grayps/
(noun)

Another name for the type of marijuana commonly referred to as purple, known for its distinctive purple hairs or coloration.

> *"Bruh stay rollin' up them grapes."*

(See also: Dank, Purple)

Grimmy

/grim-ee/
(noun)

A marijuana cigarette laced with crack cocaine.

> *"Bruh was off a grimmy, lookin' stuck."*

(See also: Cavi, Sweet One)

Grinding

/gryn-din/
(verb)

Engaging in street-level drug sales, typically through hand-to-hand transactions. The term can also refer to any form of consistent, focused hustle, where someone stays active and finds a way to get ahead by any means.

> *"Bruh out there grinding on the block every day."*

Grip

/grip/
(noun)

A large sum of money.

> *The term is likely derived from the way one's hand grips a thick stack of cash.*
>
> *"That thang cost a grip."*

(See also: D-Boy Knot)

Gucci

/goo-chee/
(adjective)

Good or "all good," often used to express that everything is fine or satisfactory.

> *"Everything's Gucci; don't worry about it."*

(See also: It's All Good)

Gurpin'

/gur-pin/
(verb)

To be high or intoxicated, typically from weed, pills, or other substances. Often implies a heavy or visibly altered state.

> *"Bruh was gurpin' off them thizzles last night."*

Half Thang
/haf thang/
(noun)

Half a kilogram of cocaine.

> "They caught cuzzo wit a half thang, he might be up outta here."

(See also: Thang)

The Hall
/thuh hawl/
(noun)

Juvenile hall or juvenile jail.

> "Bra solid, I met him in The Hall back in the day."

Hammer
/ham-er/
(noun)

A gun or firearm.

> "He actin' extra bold cause he got that hammer on him."

(See also: Cannon, Thang, Thumper)

Handles

/han-dlz/
(noun)

Skill or control, especially with one's hands; often used to describe someone with notable ability. The term is associated with handlebars, referencing mastery.

> *"He got handles behind the wheel, no question."*

(See also: Barz)

Hands

/handz/
(noun)

Skill and effectiveness in physical fighting, or the act of using that skill to strike or beat someone, often implying dominance in the altercation. Can also refer more broadly to ability or finesse in hands-on activities.

> *"You might not wanna run up on bra, he got hands."*
>
> *"You should let bra cut you, he got hands."*

(See also: Barz, Handles, Hands & Feet)

Hands & Feet

/handz an feet/
(noun phrase)

A phrase used to emphasize the severity of a physical beatdown, suggesting a person was thoroughly attacked using both fists and kicks. Often implies total domination in a fight.

> *"They caught him slippin' and put hands and feet on him."*

(See also: Hands, Molly Whopped, Mopped, Scrape)

Hater

/hay-ter/
(noun)

A person who habitually criticizes, downplays, or speaks negatively about others in an attempt to diminish their success, confidence, or reputation; usually out of jealousy, resentment, competition, or insecurity, and often offering unsolicited criticism. The term implies that the motive is not genuine concern or constructive feedback, but rather a desire to see someone do worse, feel less confident, or lose status. The antithesis of *player*.

> Shortened form of "Player Hater."
>
> "He don't even know me, but always got my name in his mouth; straight hater."

(See also: Hatin', Player Hater)

Hatin'

/hay-tin/
(verb)

Speaking or acting with negative intent toward someone's success, confidence, or reputation, usually out of envy or insecurity. Unlike offering genuine criticism, it implies an attempt to tear someone down rather than build them up.

> "They was hatin' on her just 'cause she came up."

(See also: Player Hate, Player Hater, Salt Your Game)

Havin' It

/hav-in it/
(phrase)

Possessing a significant amount of money.

> "Bra been banked up for a long time, he out here havin' it."

(See also: Banked Up, Gettin' It)

Hecka

/hek-uh/
(adverb)

A censored form of "Hella;" meaning "a lot" or "extremely."

> "We went to Disneyland last month, we had hecka fun."

(See also: Hella)

Heem

/heem/
(noun)

An emphatic form of "him," used to describe a person, thing, or experience as superior, authentic, or exemplary. Can also refer to Hennessy cognac.

> "Oh yeah, that's heem right there."

> "Pour up some of that good heem and let's chop it up."

HELLA

Few words carry as much regional weight as *hella*. A versatile intensifier rooted in Bay Area culture, particularly associated with East Bay speech, *hella* is used to intensify an adjective or adverb (similar to "extremely") or to express a large quantity (equivalent to "a lot"). Believed to have its origins in the lexicon of 1970s Black Oakland, the term is noted for its flexibility and is used informally to modify various parts of speech.

The exact etymology remains debated. Some trace it to a contraction of "hell of a," while others suggest it evolved from "a hell of a lot of." Regardless of its precise origins, by the 1980s and 1990s, hella had become deeply embedded in Bay Area vernacular, spreading outward from Oakland through the region's schools, streets, and eventually its music.

What makes hella distinctive is not just its function but its geography. The word operates as a kind of linguistic passport, immediately identifying the speaker as Northern Californian. Use it in Southern California and you'll likely draw comment; use it anywhere outside the state and you might need to explain yourself. This regional exclusivity has given hella an almost tribal significance, a small word that carries substantial cultural weight.

Despite its widespread adoption and cultural acceptance in everyday conversation, hella remains closely tied to its East Bay identity and is widely regarded as the definitive slang term most associated with the region. It has appeared in music, film, and television, yet somehow retains its authenticity, never quite crossing into the territory of overexposure that strips slang of its meaning.

Hexa

/hek-suh/
(adverb)

A child's adaptation of "hecka," which is a censored form of "hella," used to express a large amount or high degree of something.

> Sometimes playfully phrased as "hexady."
>
> "That's hexa cool!"

(See also: Extra, Hecka, Hella)

Hexady

/hek-suh-dee/
(adverb)

A child's adaptation of *hecka*, which is a censored form of *hella*, used to express a large amount or high degree of something.

> "That's hexady cool!"

(See also: Extra, Hecka, Hella)

High Power

/hy pow-er/
(adjective)

Exaggerating, fabricating, or overstating one's status, lifestyle, or importance; often used to call out someone for putting on, lying, or creating a false impression.

> "Knock it off bra, you high power frontin' right now."

(See also: 2 On The 10, Lie To Kick It, Put It On Thick)

Highside
/hy-syd/
(verb)

To show off or act superior, typically by flaunting possessions or achievements, but often done in a less offensive or harmful manner compared to "side bust."

> "Bruh hit the corner by Ben's Burger, on gold one's, straight highsidin'."

(See also: Flossin')

Hit
/hit/
(verb)

To experience a significant gain or loss, especially of money. Commonly used in gambling, dice games, or hustling to describe either catching a win or taking a loss. Context determines whether it refers to winning or losing.

> "He hit for ten racks at the tables."

(See also: Struck, Stung)

Hit A Lick
/hit uh lik/
(verb phrase)

Financial gain, often acquired through illicit means such as theft or robbery.

> "The streets is dead, everybody tryna hit a lick."

(See also: Laid Down)

Hit Me On The Hip

/hit mee own-duh hip/
(phrase)

A request to be contacted via a pager, also known as a beeper. Common from the mid-1980s through the early 2000s as a standard way to stay reachable before the widespread adoption of cell phones.

> *Precursor to "Tap In."*
>
> *Originates from the beeper era, when pagers were often worn at the hip. As pagers fell out of use, the expression largely disappeared from everyday speech.*
>
> *"I'ma be floatin' around yo area later; hit me on the hip."*

(See also: Hit My Line, Tap In)

Hit My Line

/hit my lyn/
(verb phrase)

A request for someone to call or text. A way of asking someone to contact you via phone.

> *"It's all to the good, bra; hit my line when you touch down."*

(See also: Hit Me On The Hip, Tap In)

Hit The Strip

/hit thuh strip/
(verb phrase)

To cruise or participate in the social scene along Foothill Boulevard in Oakland, specifically the stretch known as "the strip" or "the Foothill strip." Typically involves showing off cars, socializing, and being seen by others.

> Also phrased as "ride the strip."
>
> "The crew used to hit the strip every weekend and highside."

(See also: The Strip)

Hittin' Corners

/hit-in korn-erz/
(verb phrase)

Moving from place to place, often while driving. Can refer to running errands, making multiple stops, or cruising around the neighborhood or city. Often used to describe casual motion or handling small tasks while out and about.

> "I ain't doin' too much, just hittin' a few corners right quick."

(See also: The Mix, Slide, Traffic)

Hittin' It

/hit-in it/
(verb phrase)

Executing dance moves with strong rhythm, precision, and timing. Often used to describe someone dancing exceptionally well, especially when staying perfectly on beat or showcasing impressive skill.

> *"My little niece can dance hella good. On mommas, that little girl be hittin' it."*

(See also: Giggin')

Hoe Trusta

/hoh trust-uh/
(noun)

A man who places undue faith, trust, or confidence in a woman, often to a fault or to his own detriment. This can include believing in her words, character, or intentions despite evidence to the contrary, defending her against friends and family, or even risking his safety or well-being for her.

> *"Bruh turned into a straight hoe trusta, takin' her word over everybody else's."*

Holla

/hah-luh/
(verb)

To initiate contact with someone, whether in a flirtatious, conversational, or general sense. Depending on context, holla can suggest making a romantic approach, striking up a conversation, or simply reaching out.

> "Holla at me later on, bro."
>
> "She the finest at the school. I been tryin' to holla."

(See also: Chop It Up, Get At, Tap In)

Honey Boom

/huh-nee boom/
(exclamation)

An exclamation typically made by women, meaning nothing specific but showing excitement.

> "Honey boom! I'm bout to kill 'em in this new dress tonight."

Hooked

/hukt/
(adjective)

Put in position or taken care of through a favor or connection. Can also mean affiliated with a group.

> Derived from the phrase "hooked up."
>
> "That's a tight cut, your barber hooked you."
>
> "He hooked wit The Mobb."

(See also: Joog, Plug)

Hop

/hop/
(noun)

A term for heroin.

> *"Bruh been off that hop since high school."*

(See also: Bomb)

Hot

/hot/
(adjective)

Very angry, or upset.

> *"On God, that outta pocket stuff she be on be havin' me hot."*

Hot One

/hot wuhn/
(noun)

A murder case, especially referring to someone on the run from law enforcement.

> *"You heard about lil bra? He just went down for a hot one."*

Hotbox

/hot-boks/
(verb, noun)

To smoke marijuana in an enclosed space with the windows or doors shut, usually in a car, allowing the smoke to accumulate and intensify the high. Can also refer to the space itself once filled with smoke, whether a car, bathroom, or similar area with no ventilation.

> *"We had to step out the hotbox, it was thick in there."*
>
> *"We was in there hotboxin' with the windows up, couldn't see nothin'."*

Hubba

/hah-luh/
(noun)

A large piece of crack cocaine, often $20 worth.

> *"Aww shut up punk, that's why yo momma smoke hubbas."*

(See also: Cream)

Hully

/hul-lee/
(verb)

To move quickly or with urgency. Often used casually to suggest picking up the pace.

> *The form "Hullies" is sometimes used in reference to the area of East Oakland known as The Hunnids (Hundreds).*
>
> *"We runnin' late we gotta hully."*

(See also: Burl, Smash)

Hunnid

/hunnid/
(adjective, noun)

A phonetic pronunciation of "hundred," used to refer to money or to emphasize realness, effort, or authenticity.

> "He slid me a hunnid just for pullin' up."
>
> "I keep it a hunnid at all times."

(See also: Thou-Wow)

Hurt

/hert/
(adjective)

Used to describe someone who appears unattractive, unkempt, or visibly dirty. Often implies poor hygiene, lack of self-care, or a generally rough appearance.

> "I ain't even gon lie, she pulled up lookin' hurt."

(See also: Doin' Bad, Thru, Thru Wit Money)

Hush Mode

/hush mohd/
(noun)

The state of being silenced or forced to stop speaking, often as a result of being checked, proven wrong, or intimidated.

> "Bruh tried to argue but got put on hush mode quick."

Hut
/hut/
(noun)

Home or place where someone stays.

> *"I'm at the hut, slide through."*

HYPHY

Before *hyphy* became synonymous with a cultural movement, it had an altogether different connotation. A phonetic alteration of *hyper,* it was originally used to describe someone who is violently aggressive, quick-tempered, or unpredictable. The term carried with it the weight of real-life consequences in the streets. To call someone hyphy was to put others on notice that this person was violent, volatile, and not to be taken lightly. Equal parts serious and sinister.

The term evolved over time. By the early 2000s, hyphy had broadened to describe anyone excited, amped up, or uninhibited. Though gradual, the transformation was not random. It accompanied the rise of a new wave coming out of the Bay, music that was active, energetic, and aggressive. The word adapted to match the moment.

Hyphy captured a particular type of freedom. A license to get stupid, go dumb, and do you. No longer centered primarily on violence, its evolution shifted the focus toward expression, individuality, and a refusal to be contained.

The word remains central to Bay Area identity, even as the movement it named has evolved. Still, to be hyphy is to tap into something essential about the region's character: unapologetic, authentic, revolutionary and unique.

THE HYPHY MOVEMENT

A Bay Area cultural movement that began to take shape around 2003, centered around fast, bass-heavy music built for dancing, sideshows, and the streets. The sound evolved from mobb music and was shaped in part by artists like Mac Dre, Keak Da Sneak, Mistah F.A.B., and E-40. Producers like Rick Rock, Traxamillion, Droop-E, and even Lil Jon, an Atlanta native, helped define the sonic architecture that powered the movement.

But hyphy wasn't just music. The movement was characterized by go dumb dancing, ghostridin' the whip, scrapers cars, sideshows, grillz, stunna shades, tall tees, and dreads (locs) swingin'. It reflected a subculture within the Bay that centered on energy, expression, and street presence.

Even artists rooted in mobb music, like Too Short and E-40, tapped into the movement's momentum and reached new levels of national exposure. Some of their most widely recognized records, like "Blow the Whistle," and "Tell Me When to Go," came during this era, bridging generations and helping to bring Bay Area music back into the mainstream conversation.

The movement was also controversial. Many residents and artists, particularly older ones, rejected being associated with what they saw as an exaggerated or silly image. Where "hyphy" had once described someone confrontational, aggressive, and prone to violence, it had shifted into something more playful, centered around dancing and "going stupid." In Oakland especially, some pushed back against the movement's broader regional branding, seeing it as a cultural blend that placed surrounding Bay cities on equal footing with what many viewed as the true epicenter of Bay culture.

The movement created a sound, look, and language that defined a generation.

I Ain't Trippin'

/i-aynt-trip-in/
(phrase)

Unbothered or unconcerned about a situation, typically a negative one. Indicates a relaxed or dismissive attitude toward something that might otherwise be upsetting. Also used to signify agreement or willingness to participate in a suggested activity, conveying a flexible, easy-going response.

"She went on and blew up, but I ain't trippin'."

"Let's go to Ben's Burger right quick." "I ain't trippin', let's do it."

(See also: It's All Good, Trippin')

I See You

/i-see-yoo/
(phrase)

An acknowledgment of someone doing something well or impressively. Often used to show recognition or give informal praise.

"Okay, you out here makin' moves, I see you."

Icey

/eye-see/
(adjective)

Something new, stylish, or appealing, often used to describe fashion.

"I'm feelin' them kicks bra, them thangs is old school icey."

In A Minute

/in uh min-it/
(phrase)

A casual way of saying goodbye or "see you later."

> "I'ma get wit you later on, bro; in a minute."

(See also: Alright Then, Be Smooth, Love Your Life)

In Me Not On Me

/in mee not on mee/
(phrase)

Used to express that one's qualities, standards, or principles are genuine and come from within, rather than being for show or appearance. Often refers to authenticity and integrity, contrasting with those who adopt the outward image or style of something without truly embodying it.

> "They just dress the part, but it's in me not on me."

In Pocket

/in pah-kit/
(phrase)

Describes behavior or actions that are appropriate, controlled, or within expected norms, often used in contrast to "outta pocket," which implies inappropriate or excessive behavior.

> "You gettin' beside yourself, you need to get back in pocket."

(See also: Outta Pocket)

In The Building
/in thuh bild-in/
(phrase)

Another way of saying feeling yourself; used to express confidence, self-assurance, or a heightened sense of presence.

> Derived from the chorus of the popular Mac Dre song "Feelin' Myself," where he raps, "I'm in the building and I'm feelin' myself."
>
> "Okay, I see you, bruh. You in the building tonight."

(See also: Feelin' Myself, Feelin' Yourself)

In The Field
/in thuh feeld/
(phrase)

Actively involved in street activities or navigating real-world, often risky, situations. Typically refers to someone engaged in hustling, street business, or other activities requiring direct involvement.

> "Bruh not out here fake thuggin', he really in the field."

(See also: Active)

In The Way

/in thuh way/
(phrase)

Typically refers to being somewhere you have no business or involving yourself in situations where you don't belong. Often used to call out someone for unnecessary presence or interference, especially civilians in street environments.

> *Considered the antithesis of "Stayin' Out The Way."*
>
> *"Bruh ain't even active like that but he always in the way."*

(See also: Stayin' Out The Way)

Indo

/in-doh/
(noun)

A type of high-quality marijuana.

> *Likely derived from "Indonesian" or possibly a twist on the strain "indica."*
>
> *"In the early 90's it was all about that indo."*

(See also: Dank, Doja)

Instantly

/in-stint-lee/
(adverb)

Immediately; without hesitation or delay, often with a sense of decisiveness or urgency, especially in situations that demand quick action or response.

> *While a standard English word, in Bay Area usage it carries a more charged, bold, and culturally specific tone, aligning with phrases that emphasize readiness and decisiveness.*
>
> "I seen suckas at the light and got on 'em instantly."
>
> "As soon as I seen her I instantly walked up to her, like 'what's hatnin.'"

(See also: All Gas No Brakes, Off Top, On Sight)

Is It Cool?

/iz it kool/
(phrase)

A casual way of asking for permission, approval, or confirmation that something is acceptable. Implies a request to proceed without conflict, or to check if a situation, person, or action is okay.

> "I'm tryna slide through later, is it cool?"

Issue

/ish-oo/
(noun)

Something rightfully owed, due, or deserved, whether money, retribution, or satisfaction.

> Commonly used in contexts involving street transactions, conflict, or sexual encounters.
>
> "I fronted him a pack, now I need to get my issue."
>
> "He crossed the wrong people, now he about to get his issue."

It's A Big Event

/its uh big ee-vent/
(phrase)

A statement attesting to the significance or importance of a situation, moment, or occasion, especially compared to the norm. Often said among friends to mark a moment that feels special or elevated.

> "Lobster tails on a Tuesday? It's a big event, oh boy!"

(See also: It's Goin' Down, It's Real Big, Lit, Oh Boy!)

It's All Bad

/its awl bad/
(phrase)

An attestation of negativity. Can mean no, a prohibition, or a warning. Used to express that a situation is unfortunate or unfavorable, often implying that it cannot be rectified or participated in.

> *The antithesis of "It's All Good." Sometimes shortened to "It's Bad."*
>
> *"You coming out tonight?" "Nah, it's all bad. Moms said I can't go."*
>
> *"I was tryna make it but it's bad. I got called into work."*

(See also: It's All Good)

It's All Good

/its awl good/
(phrase)

An affirmation of a positive situation. Can mean yes, give permission, or signal acceptance of an apology.

> *Sometimes shortened to "It's Good."*
>
> *"It's good, bruh. Don't even trip."*
>
> *"It's all good. We can reschedule."*

(See also: Gucci, I Ain't Trippin', It's All Bad)

It's Goin' Down

/its goh-in down/
(phrase)

Something exciting is about to happen, or currently taking place.

> "It's females everywhere in this thang, it's goin' down."

It's Nothin'

/its nuth-in/
(phrase)

Indicates something is "no problem," or of no consequence, but with an air of immense confidence, arrogance, or superiority.

> The full phrase is often expressed as "It's nothin' to a boss."
>
> "I dropped five racks on the table, in her face; it's nothin' to a boss."

It's Real Big

/its reel big/
(phrase)

Indicates that something is of considerable importance or has a significant impact, emphasizing the scale or intensity of a situation, occasion, or event.

> Often preceded or followed by "Oh Boy!"
>
> "We turnin' up tonite, it's real big, oh boy!"

(See also: It's A Big Event, It's Goin' Down, Lit, Oh Boy!)

J Cat
/jay-kat/
(noun)

Someone who is mentally slow, foolish, or unstable, often showing odd or irrational behavior.

> *The term likely originates from prison slang, specifically Santa Rita County Jail, where it's linked to "JHC" or "jacket," a reference to a straitjacket, indicating a lack of mental clarity or stability.*

> "You sound like a straight J Cat talkin' like that."

(See also: Cat, Cat Off)

Jacked
/jakd/
(adjective)

Related to or derived from "jacked up"; meaning "messed up" or badly done, typically in reference to a haircut or hairstyle. Can also refer to being pulled over or caught by the police.

> "I was almost to the house and got jacked sky high on 73rd."

> "That new barber pushed yo line back to kingdom come, breh; you got jacked."

(See also: Blurped)

Jackin' Ya Slacks

/jak-in yuh slaks/
(verb phrase)

A gesture or expression similar to poppin' ya collar, but related to pants or personal style from the waist down. Often used to convey confidence, pride, or to draw attention to one's fashion, status, or swagger. Can also be used metaphorically to signify self-assurance or showing up boldly.

> "Bruh pulled up clean and bounced out jackin' his slacks."

(See also: Pop Your Collar)

Janky

/jang-kee/
(adjective)

Used to describe something low-quality, unreliable, poorly made, or suspicious. Often said about objects, setups, or situations that seem sketchy or don't work right.

> Sometimes shortened to "jank" in casual use.
>
> "Bruh sold me a janky phone, it don't even hold a charge."

(See also: Bootsie, Bunk)

Jaw Jackin'

/jaw jak-in/
(verb phrase)

Talking excessively. Similar in meaning to Jawsin', though not always implying gossip.

> "Quit all that jaw jackin' and get to the point."

(See also: Breathin', Bumpin' Ya Gums, Jawsin')

Jawsin'

/jaw-zin/
(verb)

Talking excessively, often gossiping.

> "She always jawsin' about somebody business."

(See also: Breathin', Bumpin' Ya Gums, Jaw Jackin')

Joog

/juhg/
(noun, verb)

A deal, discount, or clever scheme to acquire something for less or for free. Also refers to the act of finessing, hustling, or skillfully maneuvering to one's advantage, whether by securing a deal, getting over on someone, or offering a hook-up.

> "I got these kicks for the low, straight joog."
>
> "He jooged his way into the VIP section."

Juiced

/joost/
(adjective)

Feeling anticipatory excitement or hype. Can describe being excited about an upcoming event, energized by music, or highly motivated in response to a situation.

> "Bruh got juiced when his song came on."

(See also: Hyphy)

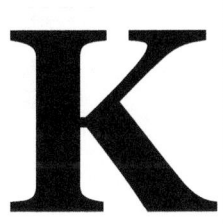

Keep It Funky
/keep it fung-kee/
(phrase)

To be completely honest or transparent, even if it's uncomfortable or offensive. Similar to keep it real, it emphasizes truthfulness without sugarcoating, especially in direct or confrontational situations.

> *"You tryna holla at my baby momma, bra? Keep it funky."*

Keep It Lit
/keep it lit/
(phrase)

An expression meaning to keep something going, stay active, or maintain an upbeat, energetic vibe.

> *"We gon' keep it lit all night."*

Keep It Player
/keep it play-er/
(phrase)

A request or reminder to maintain composure, move with integrity, or handle a situation with class and poise. The phrase reflects the mindset and principles of a true player.

> *"Don't trip off what she said, just keep it player."*

(See also: Mack, Player)

Kick

/kik/
(noun, verb)

A kilogram, often in the context of drug transactions. Can also mean to converse or communicate, especially in a compelling or persuasive way, similar to spit.

> "It's lookin' ugly, he got caught wit six kicks."
>
> "That was some good game you was kickin' last night."

(See also: Spit, Thang)

Kick It

/kik it/
(verb phrase)

Relaxing or hanging out, either with others or alone, often used in reference to casual socializing or dating.

> "What's good, boo? When we gonna kick it?"

Kick Me Down

/kik mee down/
(verb phrase)

A direct request, often a demand, to be paid, compensated, or given a cut. Typically used when money is owed, expected, or shared.

> "Kick me down for them tacos you ordered."

(See also: Break Bread, Cash Me Out, Run Mine)

Kick One

/kik wun/
(phrase)

Speeding away to evade the police, potentially initiating a high-speed chase.

> "5-0 came outta nowhere; we had to kick one."

Kickstand

/kik-stand/
(noun)

A life sentence in prison.

> *Derived from the "L" in "25 with an L" (25 to life), referencing the L-shape of a bike's kickstand.*
>
> "Just got some bad news; they hit lil cuz wit the kickstand this morning."

(See also: All Day, "L", Washed)

Kill Game

/kil gaym/
(phrase)

A directive to immediately stop a conversation or change the subject, usually because someone nearby should not overhear it, such as a child, outsider, or the person being discussed.

> *Often followed by or paired with "Talk Baseball."*
>
> "There go the supervisor, kill game."

(See also: Talk Baseball)

Knock

/nak/
(noun)

Loud, bass-heavy sound associated with music or the system playing it. Also used as a verb to describe playing or replaying music, especially tracks that hit with strong bass or impact. The term can also refer to a customer in a drug transaction, or used more broadly, a paying customer in any context. In dating, it describes successfully engaging or persuading a woman, such as sparking interest, getting a number, or setting up a future connection.

> *Rooted in pimp culture, the dating usage is short for "knocked off" or "knocked over."*
>
> *"This whole album knock, got the trunk slappin."*
>
> *"Knock that last song again, that one go crazy."*
>
> *"He knocked a bad one at the kickback last night."*
>
> *"My knock just pulled up; I'll be right back."*
>
> *"You gettin' skinny, bruh; you lookin' like a knock."*

(See also: Beat, Bump, Dope Fiend, Slap)

Knock On Me

/nak on mee/
(verb phrase)

An assertion of one's turn in a sales rotation.

> *Often related to street sales.*
>
> *"You got the last one, it's knock on me."*

Knocked Down

/nakt down/
(phrase)

To be murdered.

> "Lil cool lil bra got knocked down last night."

(See also: Downt, Laminated, Pop, Slumped, Smacked, Smoked)

Knocked Out

/nakt owt/
(phrase)

In a deep or heavy sleep.

> "I tried to call you last night, but you was knocked out."

(See also: Nodded)

Knockin'

/nak-in/
(verb)

Playing loud, bass-heavy music. Can also mean shooting a gun.

> "You hear that? Somebody outside knockin'."
>
> "He whipped out the thang and got to knockin' at that boi."

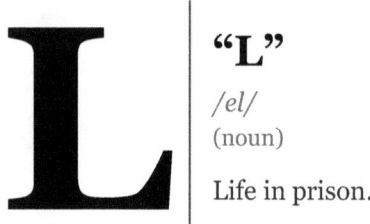

"L"
/el/
(noun)

Life in prison.

> "They gave bruh a L for that case."

(See also: All Day, Kickstand, Washed)

L.G.
/el-jee/
(initialism, noun)

Initialism for "Light Green," a potent strain of marijuana popular in the 1990s and early 2000s, named for its distinct light green appearance.

> "Back in the day, everybody was smokin' on that L.G."

La Leezy
/lah lee-zee/
(noun)

A stylized name for Los Angeles, California.

> "We mobbed all the way to La Leezy in 4 hours, on mommas."

Laced

/layss't/
(adjective)

Well-informed or educated, particularly with valuable knowledge, wisdom, or street smarts. In this sense, being laced means equipped or fortified with game. The term parallels its broader slang use of being cut or adulterated with a substance, extending here to mean infused with knowledge. It can also be used in the sense of being "laced up," like shoes tied tight, suggesting one's game is secure and properly in place.

> "Pops laced me when I was young, put me up on game."
>
> "Lace me up so I know how to move right."

(See also: Game Laced, Gamed Up)

Laid Down

/layd down/
(verb phrase)

To be robbed at gunpoint, typically forced to the ground during the act.

> "He was flashin' all that money and got laid down outside the function."

Laminated
/lam-uh-nay-tid/
(verb)

Slang for being shot to death; used to describe someone who was fatally gunned down.

> "They caught him slippin' and laminated him right there on the corner."

(See also: Downt, Knocked Down, Smacked, Smoked)

The Land
/thuh land/
(noun)

A rarely used abbreviation for "Oakland." Also refers to a state of being extremely high on marijuana.

> "Let's cut, bra, I'm ready to get back to The Land."

> "We rolled up them windows, cut that heater on, and went straight to The Land."

(See also: The "O", Oaktown, The Town)

Lash
/lash/
(verb)

To take a significant amount from an entity or situation, either through theft or a clever, assertive action; also used in dice games like craps to describe winning on the come-out roll or scoring quick consecutive wins.

> "I straight lashed em at the casino last night."

(See also: Lick)

Lavish

/lav-ish/
(adjective)

Upscale, luxurious, or extravagant. Used to describe a lifestyle, appearance, or possessions such as homes, cars, or clothing.

> Often shortened to "lav," which can also mean "all good" or "okay," as in "Is it lav?" or "It's all lav."
>
> "That penthouse lookin' lavish."
>
> "Ever since he came up, bruh been livin' lavish."
>
> "She said we straight. It's all lav."

(See also: Saucy)

Lavishly Coordinated

/lav-ish-lee kor-di-nay-tid/
(adjective)

Well put together; immaculately styled or arranged. Often used to describe someone whose outfit, accessories, or overall appearance is impressively matched, clean, and deliberate.

> "Bruh showed up lavishly coordinated from the hat to the kicks."

(See also: Fitted)

Leaked
/leekt/
(verb)

Made to bleed, often from being punched. Can also describe bleeding caused by a cut, shot, or other injury.

> "Fired on that boi like boop, bop, leaked him off top."

(See also: Leakin')

Leakin'
/lee-kin/
(verb)

Lacking awareness or attentiveness, often by failing to observe surroundings, being careless, or forgetting something. Can also describe being unprepared, the absence of something necessary or essential, or risking the loss of something important (closely related to slippin'). In some contexts, it specifically refers to being without a firearm, leaving one exposed or unprotected. The term can also literally mean bleeding.

> "Bruh left his keys in the whip, straight leakin'."
>
> "You out here leakin' foo, not even watchin' who behind you."
>
> "He slid to the block leakin', no thang on him."

(See also: Slippin')

Left Hangin'

/left hayn-gin/
(verb phrase)

To be ignored or refused when offering a dap, handshake, or gesture, leaving one's outstretched hand suspended. Often experienced as deliberate disrespect or rudeness, signaling that the person leaving you hangin' does not want to associate with you at all. By extension, can also describe being abandoned or left without expected help or support.

> "Bruh really trippin'. I tried to dap him up, he left me straight hangin'."

Left Stankin'

/left stayn-kin/
(verb phrase)

Killed and left for dead, typically in a violent or street-related context. Refers to the odor of a decomposing body, emphasizing both the finality and brutality of the act. The variation leave you stankin' is often used as a threat.

> "They dump his body in Grass Valley, left that boi stankin'."

(See also: Knocked Down, Laminated, Smacked)

Leg Check

/leg chek/
(noun)

A non-lethal demonstration of aggression, punishment, or warning, carried out by shooting someone in the leg, intended to harm but not to kill.

> "Bra must've got fed up, he pulled out the thang and leg checked that boi."

(See also: Demo)

Let It Drip

/let it drip/
(verb phrase)

To shoot a gun, often referring to the use of an automatic weapon. Implies continuous or repeated firing.

> "Bruh pulled up wit that big thang and let it drip."

(See also: Aired Out, Lit Up)

Let That Go

/let that goh/
(phrase)

An instruction to move on, drop an issue, or discontinue an undesirable action or behavior.

> "Bruh, that argument old. Let that go."

Lick

/lik/
(noun, verb)

A plan or opportunity to make fast money, often through robbery or setup. Can also refer to the person being targeted. The term is also used in craps to describe a win, typically on the come-out roll.

> "Boi, you walkin' around wit all that jewelry on lookin' like a lick."

(See also: Hit A Lick)

Lie To Kick It

/lye tuh kik it/
(phrase)

Being dishonest to gain favor or acceptance.

> "It's a well-known fact that you still a virgin bra, you ain't gotta lie to kick it."

(See also: 2 On The 10, High Power, Put It On Thick)

Lightweight

/lyt-wayt/
(adverb)

Somewhat; kind of; to a certain extent. Often used to modestly downplay an achievement, quality, or feeling, even when the subject may actually be significant or intense.

> "I heard you doin' ya thang at the new job!" "Yeah, lightweight..."
>
> "We was lightweight turnt up at the club last night."
>
> "She lightweight feelin' me, I can tell."

Lightweight Jammin'

/lyt-wayt jam-in/
(verb phrase)

A playful way of saying someone is enjoying music, often by playing it loudly, dancing to it, or participating in its creation. The use of jammin' is intentionally old-fashioned, often said with humor or irony to reference a bygone era of musical expression.

> "He in the back with the speaker on blast, lightweight jammin'."

(See also: Lightweight)

Like Whaattt

/lyk whaat/
(interjection)

An emphatic expression of confidence, pride, or certainty. Often used to punctuate a statement, moment, or accomplishment with energy or attitude. Typically signals that the speaker is asserting their presence unapologetically, with a slightly confrontational undertone.

> "We yanked up in the van ten deep and bounced out, like whaattt."

(See also: Ayyy, Yadadamean, Yeee!, You Feel Me)

Lil

/lil/
(adjective)

A versatile term derived from "little," but not exclusively used to describe size. It can refer to familiarity or endearment, or simply act as a casual modifier in various contexts. Often used to minimize a person, a thing, or an action, whether deliberately or unintentionally.

> "I guess she feelin' herself 'cause she just opened up her lil business."

Lil Mama

/lil mah-muh/
(noun)

A casual term for a woman or girl, often used in reference to someone petite or youthful in appearance. Can be affectionate, flirtatious, or simply descriptive depending on context.

> "Lil mama over there lookin' decent."

(See also: Baby Girl)

Line

/lyn/
(noun)

A connection, point of contact, or channel of communication. Often refers to access to someone, their phone, or their attention. Can imply direct contact, pursuit, or access to something or someone of value.

> "I got a line on some work if you still need it."

> "Lil Momma steady askin' about you. She on yo line bra."

(See also: On Your Line, Tap In)

Lit

/lit/
(adjective)

High energy or exciting, especially when referring to a party, event, or situation. Can also describe someone who is intoxicated or high.

> *Sometimes stylized as "litty" (/lit-ee/) for added emphasis or playful effect.*
>
> *"That function was lit last night."*
>
> *"Bruh off the thizz, he big lit."*

(See also: Juiced, Thizzin', Yankin')

Lit Up

/lit uhp/
(verb phrase)

Shot multiple times, typically with emphasis on the number of bullets, or intensity of gunfire. Can refer to a person, vehicle, building, dwelling, or any other target being riddled with bullets.

> *"They slid through and lit the whole whip up."*

(See also: Aired Out)

Liv Mo

/lyv moh/
(noun)

Livermore, California. A shortened local nickname used casually in Bay Area circles.

> *"She from Liv Mo but always in The Town."*

Loaded
/loh-did/
(adjective)

Intoxicated from drugs or alcohol. Often used to describe someone whose speech, movement, or judgment is noticeably impaired.

> "Bruh was way too loaded to even think about driving."

(See also: Gurpin', Lit, On One, Out My Body, Tweakin')

The Longest
/thuh lawng-uhst/
(phrase)

Used to emphasize an unnecessarily extended period, often in the context of waiting, delays, or long absences.

> Short for "the longest time."

> "Damn, you had me waitin' out here for the longest."

(See also: Sucka Standby)

Louisville
/loo-ee-vil/
(noun)

A short, even haircut style.

> Often shortened to "Louie."

> "He wanted a fade, but pops made him get a Louie."

(See also: Quo Vadis)

Love

/luhv/
(noun)

A generous or extra portion of something, typically given freely or with good intention. Often used to describe an act of kindness or a hookup.

> *"He filled my plate with extra mac and cheese, straight love."*

(See also: Hooked)

Love Your Life

/luv yo life/
(phrase)

A farewell expression used between close friends or family to wish well, offer safety, and affirm care before parting. Carries a tone of warmth, respect, and mutual solidarity.

> *"See ya in a minute lil bra, be smooth. I love yo life."*

(See also: Alright Then, Be Smooth, In A Minute)

Loved One

/luv-d wuhn/
(noun)

A term of address used in a familiar, respectful, or affectionate way, similar to "bro" or "homie," often as a casual greeting or when speaking to a friend.

> "Ayy, check this out, loved one, it ain't cool to park right there."
>
> "What's good, loved one? What you got up for the day?"

L's

/elz/
(noun)

A valid driver's license.

> "Bruh finally got his L's so he can slide now."

(See also: Elroy)

Mack

/mack/
(noun, verb)

Often considered to be an advanced player with elevated game. Someone who has refined his approach, often expanding his game beyond traditional street hustles and finding ways to generate income across multiple avenues. In the hierarchy of the game, a mack isn't necessarily above or below a pimp. The term is subjective and often debated, based on one's personal understanding and perspective. Still, in many circles, the mack is regarded as a more evolved figure; someone who has ascended to higher game. While a pimp is typically focused on one dedicated lane, the mack operates more like a jack of all trades, expanding his reach without abandoning the structure, principles, or discipline of the game. As a verb, to mack means to run game smoothly, to seduce or persuade skillfully.

The word gained traction through the 1973 film The Mack, filmed in Oakland and widely regarded as one of the most authentic portrayals of the player lifestyle. The film drew from real people and places, with strong influence from local figure Frank Ward and his brothers, often credited with introducing the term "mack" into the Bay Area lexicon. Known for multiple hustles, the Wards embodied the broader meaning of the term: not just pimping, but mastering various forms of influence and enterprise.

"Bruh ain't just a player, he a real mack, playin' on another level."

(See also: Game, Player)

The Mack God

/thuh mack god/
(noun)

A figurative force believed to govern over fairness, order, and consequence within the game. Often invoked when someone disregards the principles of playerism, as well as when someone upholds them with integrity and class. Believed to reward those who conduct themselves honorably and reprimand those in violation.

> *While not necessarily a deity in the traditional sense, the Mack God represents the unseen force of order and balance, felt instinctually in the weight of decisions that separate those who play the game from those who cross it.*
>
> "He violated The Game, now he gettin' what's comin' to him. That's The Mack God."

(See also: Mack, Mack Hand)

Mack Hand

/mak hand/
(noun)

A firm, no-nonsense approach used to check or correct a woman's behavior, typically in response to something out of line or disrespectful. Often refers to maintaining structure in a relationship through the implementation of discipline, authority, and elevated game.

> "She was trippin', so I had to put the mack hand down."

(See also: Mack)

Mail

/mayl/
(noun)

A term used to refer to money.

> "She a real hustler, out here havin' mail."

(See also: Bank, Paper, Skrilla)

Main

/mayn/
(noun)

The primary woman of a man who's entertaining multiple ladies. Implies status, consistency, or rank within a romantic hierarchy.

> *Derived from "main broad," a phrase used to distinguish the most important, primary, or central woman.*

> "He got a few girls, but everybody know who his main is."

Mainy

/may-nee/
(adjective)

Ruthless, crazy, or exhibiting wild, often extreme, or unpredictable behavior.

> "Blud was a certified beast back in the day. Straight mainy."

(See also: Hyphy, Sic)

Major

/may-jer/
(adjective)

Signifies someone or something of high importance, stature, or influence. Often refers to a person, group, or event regarded as powerful or significant.

> Commonly paired with "factor" to emphasize influence.
>
> "We out here doin the damn thang, in a major way."

Major Factor

/may-jer fak-ter/
(noun)

A highly influential individual, often with power, money, or status. Commonly used to describe someone who plays a central role in the streets or drug trade, especially at a high level. The term emphasizes both reach and significance.

> "He ain't just out here hustlin', he a major factor."

(See also: Factor)

Mando

/man-doh/
(adjective)

Used to describe something required, necessary, or without question.

> Short for "mandatory."
>
> "They gotta bump that Dre before the party over. That's mando."

Marinate
/mare-uh-nayt/
(verb)

To relax or chill; or to ponder, consider, or contemplate a situation.

> Similar to "sleep on it."
>
> "I'm just gon' marinate at the crib for a while."
>
> "Marinate on what I said and get back to me tomorrow."

Mark
/mark/
(noun)

A person who is easily intimidated or considered a coward, often targeted for being perceived as weak.

> "I went to junior high wit bra, he been a mark."

(See also: Busta, Poodle, Sucka)

Mayne
/mayn/
(interjection, noun)

A phonetic variation of man, commonly used for emphasis or as a conversational filler.

> Not typically used when describing a man but often used to address others or to add emphasis to a statement.
>
> "We goin' straight to the top, mayne."

Mean Mug

/meen muhg/
(verb, noun)

A hostile, unfriendly, often aggressive facial expression, used to convey disapproval, intimidation, confrontation, or general displeasure. Can refer to the act of directing such a look at someone or simply wearing the expression.

> "Why you mean muggin' me like that?"
>
> "He walked in with a mean mug, ready to start trippin'."

Mil-Ticket

/mil-tik-it/
(noun)

A term for one million dollars, representing a major financial milestone or life-changing sum.

> Often shortened to "ticket" in casual usage.
>
> Derived from "meal ticket," a metaphor for financial arrival or access, reinforcing the idea of wealth as a "ticket" to success.
>
> "Bruh touched his first mil-ticket and ain't looked back since."
>
> "He said he wasn't movin' 'less it was a ticket on the table."

(See also: Band, Rack, Thou-Wow)

Million Dollar Spot

/mil-yun dol-er spot/
(noun)

A drug turf known for producing exceptionally high profits, sometimes literally generating millions of dollars and/or producing a multitude of high earners and/or millionaires. Controlling such a spot often signifies status, power, or dominance in street business.

> "The turf was rollin' non-stop back in the day; straight million dollar spot."

Miss Me

/mis mee/
(verb phrase)

Used to dismiss a suggestion, behavior, or assumption that is unwelcome, absurd, or out of line. Implies that the speaker wants no part of what's being offered or implied. A way of rejecting something outright.

> "You on some 'ole other s*** today; miss me wit all that."

(See also: Bent)

Mission

/mish-in/
(noun)

An endeavor or destination requiring a long, often undesirable or unnecessary journey. Frequently used to describe lengthy travel or errands, especially those perceived as inconvenient.

> "I'll give you a ride if you need me to, but that's a mission."

(See also: Strike)

The Mix
/thuh miks/
(noun)

The streets or the general environment of street life, including its associated activities, dynamics, and risks. Being "in the mix" implies involvement in street culture, whether through hustling, socializing, or navigating its challenges.

> "He been in the mix since he was young."

(See also: Active, In The Field)

The Mobb
/thuh mahb/
(noun)

A loosely defined collective within Bay Area street culture, representing those recognized as connected, respected, or actively engaged in the life. Membership is fluid and determined not by formal initiation, leadership, or hierarchy, but by social perception, reputation, and one's affiliations within the community. An abstract concept, similar in nature to an "in crowd," but rooted in street credibility and cultural belonging rather than social status alone.

> *The term carries historical weight in Oakland, most notably through the 6-9 Mob, a prominent street organization led by Felix Mitchell during the 1980s. M.O.B., an acronym for "My Other Brother," reflected the familial bond among its members. The name later reemerged as the moniker for a notable Oakland rap collective, a supergroup of prominent local artists, reinforcing its cultural presence across generations.*
>
> "You got me twisted; you must don't know I'm in the mobb."

(See also: Mobbin', Mobligated, On The Mobb, Solid)

MOBB MUSIC

A style of rap music originating in the independent Bay Area scene. Defined by heavy synthesizer basslines, 808 drum patterns, and lyrical themes centered around street life and experience. Often characterized by a fusion of gangster and player perspectives over productions influenced by 1970s and '80s Soul, Funk, and R&B. Regarded as a foundational influence on genres like Hyphy, Trap, and G-Funk.

Although the term Mobb Music is widely credited to E-40, the musical foundation of the sound traces back to Too Short's mid-1980s recordings. Other defining elements include spooky textures, melodic components, and live instrumentation.

While the specifics of its origins vary, consensus typically includes among its early pioneers the previously mentioned Too Short, and E-40 & The Click, as well as Mac Dre, along with other notable artists such as 415, Dangerous Dame, MC Ant, Poohman, and Spice 1. Master P, who lived in and claimed Richmond during this era, absorbed the Mobb sound and Bay hustle before building No Limit into a national empire.

Other prominent Mobb artists emerged throughout the early and mid-1990s, including RBL Posse, Mac Mall, C-Bo, 3X Krazy, Dru Down, Totally Insane, The Delinquents, Messy Marv, Askari X, Bad-N-Fluenz, Luniz, JT The Bigga Figga, and Seagram.

Notable producers credited with shaping the sound include Ant Banks, Studio Ton, DJ Daryl, Khayree, and Mike Mosley & Sam Bostic. Additional producers who helped solidify the genre's sound through the early to mid-1990s include E-A-Ski, Tone Capone, One Drop Scott, T.C., Hook Me Mike D, and others.

Mobbin'

/mah-bin/
(verb)

To move with an uncompromising attitude of purpose and force. Sometimes alone, but often in a group. While often involving crime or confrontation, it also describes a code-bound mindset, driven by assertiveness and deliberate action, without concern for consequence, permission, or approval. The term can also refer to driving fast or aggressively, or more casually, to riding or moving around, carrying the same spirit of motion without hesitation.

> *"It wasn't about money, it was about mobbin'."*

(See also: Slide, Smash, Smobbin')

Mobby

/mah-bee/
(noun)

A car, typically mid-level in quality. Considered more reliable and presentable than a bucket, though not luxury. Often refers to a vehicle that is functional, modest, and capable of getting you from point A to B without major issue.

> *"I ain't trippin' off a rental, I'll pull up in the mobby and still get respect."*

(See also: Bucket)

Mobe

/mohb/
(noun)

A cell phone; one's personal mobile device.

> Short for "mobile phone."
>
> "He stay glued to the mobe."

(See also: Mobil)

Mobil

/moh-buhl/
(noun)

Possessing transportation; able to drive.

> Also short for "mobile phone."
>
> "I just got my whip fixed, I'm back mobil."
>
> "She hit me on the mobil, late night."

(See also: Mobe)

Mobligated

/mahb-lih-gay-tid/
(adjective)

Bound or compelled by loyalty, allegiance, or commitment, whether to one's immediate circle or, more broadly, to the universally accepted rules, standards, and codes of the streets. Obligated to the mobb.

> The noun form "mobligation" is also used to describe the principle itself.
>
> "Bruh known to stand on business; straight mobligated to the hood."

(See also: Mobbin')

Molded

/mohld-id/
(adjective)

Incorrect or mistaken to the point of embarrassment.

> *Likely derived from the association of green, the color of mold, with embarrassment.*
>
> "See, you thought you knew what you was talkin' about and got molded."

Molly Whopped

/mah-lee wahpt/
(verb)

Hit hard or beaten severely.

> "Bruh went up there doin' too much talkin' and end up gettin' molly whopped."

(See also: Mopped)

Mopped

/mahpt/
(adjective)

Badly beaten or defeated.

> *Likely derived from the phrase "mop the floor with."*
>
> "Bruh got mopped in front of everybody."

(See also: Molly Whopped, Scrape)

Motion

/mo-shun/
(noun)

Social momentum, recognition, or influence, often indicating rising status or increasing validation from others.

> "Bruh got real motion right now, everybody tryna tap in."

Mouthpiece

/mouth-pees/
(noun)

The ability to speak well; not just in diction, but through intellect, persuasion, and clarity of expression. Suggests a verbal finesse, often combining articulate speech with knowledge, wisdom, and understanding, enabling communication that effectively navigates and influences people, situations, and circumstances through words.

> "That boi got mouthpiece outta this world."

(See also: Game, Spit Game)

Move Mean

/moov meen/
(verb phrase)

To operate with strategic finesse and a calculated combination of power, intention, and force. Often describes conduct marked by confidence, skill, and deliberate, intellectual precision.

> "Thangs gettin' way too real out here, what time it is is to be movin' mean."

(See also: Rockin')

Movin'

/moo-vin/
(adjective)

Energetic, exciting, or socially active. Used to describe something with good energy, heavy traffic, or a lively vibe. Often said about parties, functions, or places with a lot goin' on.

> *"First Friday was lit last night. That thang was dumb-ass movin'."*

Mustard & Mayonnaise

/mus-terd and may-uh-nayz/
(noun)

A vogue tire featuring a whitewall with yellow trim. The name plays on the contrast in colors, "mustard" for the yellow edge and "mayonnaise" for the whitewall.

> *"Bruh pulled up in the Caddy on mustard and mayonnaise."*

N.S.O.
/en ess oh/
(initialism, noun)

Initialism for North Side Oakland. Occasionally used, more often in writing or graffiti, to represent North Oakland.

Rarely spoken in conversation.

"Bro been reppin' N.S.O. since way back."

(See also: E.S.O., The North Pole, W.S.O.)

Nade
/nay-d/
(noun)

A San Francisco term for potent marijuana. Often used to emphasize high quality or intensity.

Likely derived from "grenade" to suggest something green, and explosively strong.

"All we smoke is straight nade."

(See also: Bomb, Cryp)

Nathan

/nay-thin/
(noun)

A deliberate variation in the pronunciation of "nothing," often used to dismiss or minimize something as insignificant.

> Variant: "Nathanael" (/nay-than-yuhl/) is an exaggerated or playful form sometimes used for emphasis.
>
> "Lil Mama got me misconstrued, I ain't given her nathan."

Never That

/nev-er that/
(phrase)

An emphatic refusal or rejection. Used to express strong disagreement or to firmly deny something.

> "You think I'm finna let that slide? Never that."

No Fingerprints

/noh fing-ger-printz/
(phrase)

A statement made while performing a stylized handshake or greeting in which two people lightly tap or wiggle the backs of their fingers together as a subtle sign of agreement, recognition, or respect. The phrase conveys secrecy, discretion, and a quiet understanding that those with awareness move in relative silence.

> The words "no fingerprints" give meaning to the act, sometimes extended to "no fingerprints, no evidence," or used in a call-and-response where one person says "no fingerprints" and the other replies "no evidence."
>
> "It's nothin' to a boss, ya understand me? No fingerprints..."

(See also: Feelin' Me Fingers)

Nodded

/nod-ed/
(adjective)

In a light, unintentional sleep, often from exhaustion or deep relaxation; a state of drifting off or dozing, usually without fully lying down.

> "I ain't even hear the doorbell, I was over here nodded."

(See also: Knocked Out)

Noid

/noyd/
(adjective)

A feeling of unease, suspicion, or heightened alertness.

> Shortened form of "paranoid."
>
> "He's acting all noid, lookin' over his shoulder every few seconds."

Noodle

/noo-dl/
(noun)

A soft or cowardly person; someone seen as weak, scary, or lacking backbone. Often used to call out fake bravado or exposed vulnerability.

> Possibly a phonetic play on "poodle."
>
> "Soon as it got heated, all that talk went straight out the window. That boy a straight noodle."

(See also: Busta, Mark, Poodle, Sucka, Weenie)

The North Pole

/thuh north pole/
(noun)

North Oakland; the section of Oakland, CA located north of downtown.

> Sometimes referred to simply as "The North."
>
> "He from the North Pole, up there by Bushrod."

(See also: N.S.O., Polar Bear)

Nose Job

/nohz jahb/
(noun)

A coded term for cocaine, referencing its method of use.

> "They in the bathroom off that nose job."

(See also: Playin' Wit Your Nose)

Num

/nuhm/
(noun)

A telephone number.

> Short for "number." The Bay Area equivalent of the East Coast's "math" or "digits."

> "I seen his broad at the bar. Why she slid me the num tho?"

(See also: Line, Tap In)

Nut Up

/nuht uhp/
(verb)

To snap or explode emotionally, usually in anger or frustration. Suggests reaching a breaking point and reacting without restraint.

> "He kept on playin' 'til lil bruh finally nutted up on him."

(See also: Fake Nutty, Flash, Nutty)

Nutty

/nuht-ee/
(adjective)

An emotional outburst or moment of extreme reaction, often loud, dramatic, or unexpected. Can imply a loss of control or composure, whether genuine or exaggerated.

> "Soon as they said her name, he did a nutty in the courtroom."

(See also: Dummy, Fake Nutty, Flash, Go Dumb)

The "O"

/thuh oh/
(noun)

A nickname for Oakland, California.

> *A shortened, casual way of referring to the city, commonly used in speech and writing.*
>
> *"Bruh been reppin' The O since day one."*

(See also: The Land, Oaktown, The Town)

O.G.

/oh jee/
(noun)

A casual term used to refer to an older man, typically one significantly older than the speaker.

> *The phrase is commonly understood in other regions as "Original Gangster," but in the Bay it's often said to stand for "Older Gentleman," and is used without regard to status, experience, or social rank.*
>
> *"What's up wit you, O.G.? How you feelin'?"*

(See also: Big Bruh)

Oaktown

/oak-toun/
(noun)

A nickname for Oakland, California, popularized in the 1980s and 1990s.

> *While once widely accepted (though typically used in moderation), the term has largely fallen out of use, giving way to the more popular and enduring nickname "The Town," to which "Oaktown" served as an early, often uncredited predecessor.*
>
> *"Back in the day, some people called it Oaktown, but now it's just The Town."*

(See also: The Land, The "O", The Town)

Off

/awf/
(adjective)

Lacking financial stability, often used to describe someone going through hardship or no longer thriving. Also used to indicate deep engagement with something at a given time, such as music or a substance that is currently or was very recently consumed.

> *"He used to be on, but now he all the way off."*
>
> *"We used to be off that mobb music tuff in high school."*
>
> *"We off that Hennessy and apple juice right now, turnt up."*

(See also: Doin' Bad, Financially Embarrassed, Pockets Touchin')

Off The Hook

/awf thuh huk/
(phrase)

Good, impressive, or exciting. Often used to describe food, a party, or anything that delivers above expectations. Can also refer to something wild, heavily populated, uninhibited, or downright ridiculous depending on context.

> *"Auntie be drunk as hell, she off the hook."*
>
> *"They had oxtails, peach cobbler, the whole plate was off the hook."*

(See also: Dummy, Gas, Go Crazy, Off The Richter, Tight)

Off The Richter

/awf thuh rik-ter/
(phrase)

Used to describe something extremely good, exciting, or intense. Often applied to parties, events, or situations that go beyond the usual level.

> *Short for "off the Richter scale."*
>
> *Commonly used as a more extreme variation of "Off The Hook."*
>
> *"That function was off the Richter."*

(See also: Off The Hook)

Off Top

/awf tahp/
(phrase)

Immediately or from the beginning; "for sure."

> "We need to link up one day soon, off top."

(See also: Fasho, Instantly)

Oh Boy!

/oh boy/
(exclamation)

An exclamation used to express anticipation or excitement about something significant or impactful happening.

> Often paired with or follows "It's real big."
>
> "It's going down in a major way, it's real big, oh boy!"

Old School

/ohld skool/
(noun, adjective)

A classic car, typically from the 1960s-1970s era, usually American-made. The term can also be used to reference behaviors, styles, or phrases from the past, often in a casual way that adds a touch of nostalgia to the conversation. Frequently followed by a word, phrase, or gesture that reflects an earlier era.

> "I'm thinkin' about flippin' another old school this summer."
>
> "Unk was at the party last night old school giggin'."

On

/own/
(adjective)

A flexible term used to describe a range of active states, including financial success, intoxication, engagement, pursuit, or advantage. Can describe someone who has money or status ("he been on"), someone under the influence ("we was on last night"), someone actively doing something ("what you on today?"), or someone targeting or pursuing another, whether romantically or in conflict ("he been on her all night" or "they say they on me when they see me").

> "Bruh a major factor, he been on for years."
>
> "That Sem store Mai Tai had us on last night."
>
> "Sis been trippin' lately, I don't know what she on."
>
> "I keep catchin' her lookin', I think she on me."
>
> "They gon fasho get on him about that disrespect."

On Citas

/own see-tuhz/
(phrase)

Swearing by one's mother.

> Derived from "mamacita."
>
> "Yo lil son raw at that hoop, bra, on citas."

(See also: On Errythang, On God, On Mommas, On The Mobb)

On Errythang

/own airy-thayng/
(phrase)

An expression used to assert the truthfulness or seriousness of one's words, similar to making a solemn vow or strong declaration of sincerity or commitment.

> "I'm out here tryna get my money on, on errythang."

(See also: On Citas, On God, On Mommas, On The Mobb)

On God

/own gahd/
(phrase)

A serious affirmation or vow of truth; used to emphasize sincerity or certainty, similar to saying "I swear to God."

> "I ain't lying, on God I seen it happen just like that."

(See also: G.O.D.)

On Hit

/own hit/
(adjective)

Exceptionally good or satisfying; most often used to describe delicious food, good music, or other enjoyable experiences.

> "That gumbo was on hit, I had to get seconds."

(See also: Slap, Smackin')

On Like S***

/own lyke s***/
(adjective phrase)

In an elevated state, whether from excitement, influence, or momentum. Often describes someone active, expressive, or under the influence. Can also refer to being in an excellent, privileged, or highly favorable position.

> "The party was turnt up, everybody in there was on like s***."

(See also: On, On One)

On Line

/own lyn/
(phrase)

In possession; having product or supplies on hand.

> "It's bad right now, but I'll hit you when I'm back on line."

On Mommas

/own mah-muhz/
(phrase)

An assertive proclamation of truth; to swear by one's mother.

> Also stylized as "on my momma" to emphasize sincerity or seriousness.
>
> "Steph Curry the best shooter in the world, on mommas."

(See also: On Citas)

On My Hype

/own my hype/
(phrase)

Indicates someone is on a similar wavelength, vibe, or adopting one's style, energy, or movement.

> *Variants include: "On Your Hype," "On They Hype," etc.*
>
> *"I'm out here havin' my way, you might wanna get on my hype."*

On One

/own wun/
(phrase)

In an extreme or heightened state, whether emotionally upset, intoxicated or high, riding a streak of momentum, or actively pursuing something disruptive, challenging, or intense.

> *"Moms was on one last night, goin' off on everybody."*
>
> *"Bruh been on one all week, makin' moves nonstop."*

On Sight

/on syt/
(phrase)

Indicates an immediate intention to confront, fight, or attack someone the moment they are seen.

> *"Soon as I see you, it's on sight."*

On Some Other S***

/on sum uh-thur s***/
(adjective phrase)

Behaving in a way that's strange, unpredictable, or unreasonable; acting outside of expected norms or typical behavior.

> "Ever since she linked with them new folks, she been on some other s***."

(See also: Cat Off, Trippin', Weird)

On The Gooch

/on the gooch/
(phrase)

An affirmation of truth, similar to "for real" or "on God." Used to emphasize sincerity or confirm that something is not a lie.

> Sometimes pronounced "On the Goo-chee."
>
> Possibly derived from The Gooch, Arnold's never-seen school bully from the 1980s sitcom Diff'rent Strokes.
>
> "I jumped off the porch as a youngsta, on the goochee."

(See also: On Errythang, On God, On Mommas, On The Mobb)

On The Ground

/on thuh grownd/
(phrase)

Riding or owning a motorcycle, typically a Harley Davidson.

> "Bro just flipped a Road King, he finally on the ground."

On The Hush
/on thuh hush/
(adverb phrase)

Done quietly, discreetly, or in secret, often to avoid attention.

> "We could do a lil somethin', just keep it on the hush."

(See also: Under)

On The Mobb
/on thuh mahb/
(phrase)

A strong affirmation or oath referencing a subgroup of Bay Area culture, implying deep conviction.

> "Real talk, I gets down and dirty about mines, on the mobb."

(See also: G.O.D., The Mobb, On Errythang, On God, On Mommas, On The Gooch)

On Your Bumper
/on yer bump-er/
(phrase)

Used metaphorically to indicate that someone is being persistently pursued, pressured, or targeted, whether as a threat, warning, or sign of strong interest. It can refer to actual pursuit or someone being overly attentive, including in a romantic sense.

> "Baby from last night hit me 3 times already. She on my bumper."
>
> "They been talkin' reckless, but if we catch 'em slippin', we on they bumper."

(See also: On Your Hat, On Your Helmet, On Your Line)

On Your Hat

/on yer hat/
(phrase)

Indicates someone being targeted, whether for violence, confrontation, or reprimand. Can refer to physical retaliation or verbal chastisement.

> "I can't be late again, or the boss gon' be on my hat."

(See also: On Your Bumper, On Your Helmet, On Your Line)

On Your Helmet

/on yer hel-mit/
(phrase)

A declaration of intent to confront, attack, or harshly criticize someone. Can imply physical assault or intense verbal pressure.

> "He crossed the wrong people, they tried to get on that boy helmet."

(See also: On Your Bumper, On Your Hat, On Your Line)

On Your Line

/on yer lyn/
(phrase)

Persistent attention, contact, or pursuit from someone, whether in a romantic, social, or confrontational context. It can imply admiration, pressure, or even a looming threat, depending on the situation.

> Variants include: "On My Line," "On His Line," "On They Line," etc.
>
> "She been callin' me all day, she really on my line."
>
> "They heard what he did, now they on his line heavy."

(See also: Line, On Your Bumper, On Your Hat, On Your Helmet)

One Hunnid

/wuhn hunnid/
(phrase)

Complete honesty, reliability, or strength of character. Used to describe someone or something that is dependable, authentic, and without falsehood.

> "He kept it one hunnid the whole time."

(See also: Solid, Thou-Wow)

One Time

/wuhn tym/
(phrase)

Used to describe a single or brief instance, either as a request for a favor or in reference to something that happened quickly or just once.

> "Come on, just hook me up one time."

> "Lil bra, check it out. Lemme holla at you one time."

(See also: Hooked, Joog, One Time For The One Time, Plug)

One Time For The One Time

/wuhn tym fuh thuh wuhn tym/
(phrase)

An extension of one time, often used when requesting or referring to a deal, discount, or hook-up. Emphasizes a single, possibly special instance.

> "Let me hold somethin' bra; one time for the one time."

(See also: Hooked, Joog, One Time, Plug)

One-Hitter-Quitter

/wuhn hit-er kwit-er/
(noun)

A single punch that knocks someone out or ends a fight instantly.

> "He caught him wit a one-hitter-quitter; sent that boy night-night."

(See also: Fired On, Molly Whopped, Mopped, Stole On)

Out Here

/owt heer/
(phrase)

Indicates active involvement in the broader world or a specific situation, often used to emphasize persistence and effort.

> "I'm out here tryin' to get it; you feel me?"

Out My Body

/owt my bod-ee/
(phrase)

Extremely drunk or intoxicated. Often used to describe a state of being highly under the influence of alcohol or drugs.

> "Bruh was at the function last night out his body; on my mama."

Out The Trunk

/owt thuh truhnk/
(phrase)

Selling goods directly to consumers without major distribution; an independent hustle.

> "You know how we hustle in The Bay, straight out the trunk."

Out The Way

/owt thuh way/
(phrase)

Refers to a location that is distant, remote, or removed from one's usual area; often used when talking about someone's residence in the suburbs or farther from the city or hometown.

> "He just bought a new house out the way."

Outside

/owt-syd/
(adjective)

Actively present and engaged in the world with purpose and intention. Often used when a person is choosing visibility and showing up in public spaces after a period of absence or low visibility. Reflects a deliberate effort to assert one's presence.

> "You wasn't outside when it was really active."

> "She don't wanna be in a relationship no more, she'd rather be outside."

(See also: Traffic)

Outta Pocket

/ow-tuh pah-kit/
(adjective phrase)

Unacceptable, wrong, or out of line. Used to describe behavior that is disrespectful, inappropriate, or beyond acceptable boundaries.

> *"She sat up there for six hours without changing his diaper. Hella outta pocket."*

(See also: In Pocket)

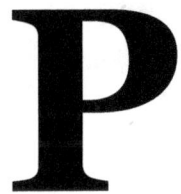

"P"
/pee/
(noun)

An abbreviation for "pimp" or "pimpin'," and occasionally used to mean player. Describes someone with game, influence, or social dominance, often in the context of dating, hustling, or street culture.

> "Bruh keep it straight P at all times."

(See also: 16, Game, Player)

P.C.
/pee-see/
(initialism, noun)

A consistent or exclusive client, often in the context of drug sales.

> Short for "Personal Customer."

> "He ain't even servin' everybody, just his P.C.s."

P.H.
/pee-aych/
(initialism, noun)

Initialism for player hater, implying someone fully embodying the qualities of a hater.

> Often phrased as "P.H. balanced" as a play on the scientific term.

> "I can't rock wit blud no more, that mark straight P.H. balanced."

(See also: Hater, Player Hate, Player Hater)

Pae Pae
/pay pay/
(noun)

Powder cocaine; a casual or playful term used to refer to it without directly saying the drug name.

> *A playful reduplication, possibly referencing "powder."*
>
> *"They was off that pae pae at the party."*

(See also: Nose Job, Pow Wow, Powda)

Paper
/pay-per/
(noun)

Money; often used to refer to cash, wealth, or financial success, especially in street culture.

> *"Bruh out here ballin'; he havin' his paper."*

(See also: Bank, Mail, Skrilla)

Papered Up
/pay-perd up/
(adjective)

Having a lot of money; doing well financially.

> *"She paid for the whole table, she out here papered up."*

(See also: Ballin', Banked Up, Caked Up, Havin' It, On)

Parking Lot Pimpin'

/par-kin laht pim-pin/
(verb phrase)

Congregating outside a club, bar, or party, to hang out, socialize, or pursue romantic interests. Often done instead of going inside, or after the event has ended.

> *"We ain't even goin' in, we just parking lot pimpin' tonight."*

Parlay

/par-lay/
(noun)

To spend time relaxing or socializing in a casual setting. Often used to describe hanging out without a specific purpose or agenda.

> *"We just parlayed at the spot all night."*

(See also: Marinate)

Peanuts To An Elephant

/pee-nuts tuh un el-uh-funt/
(phrase)

Highlights how unimportant, negligible, or easily handled something is when weighed against one's strength, resources, or experience. Carries a tone of dismissal or quiet assurance, implying the matter barely registers as a challenge.

> *"All that small stuff you talkin' bout is just peanuts to an elephant."*

(See also: Balloons To A Blimp, Small Thing To A Giant)

Pearl

/purl/
(noun, verb)

A term referring to the female genitalia, often extended to mean intercourse, usually expressed from the male perspective.

> "He stay braggin' like he pearlin' every other weekend."

Peelt

/peelt/
(verb)

A pronunciation variant of "peeled," meaning taken or stolen from. Often used to describe being robbed, stripped of belongings, or otherwise having something taken away.

> Phonetic spelling of "peeled," reflecting local pronunciation.
>
> "Bruh got peelt for his whole bankroll."

Peep

/peep/
(verb)

To notice, see, or recognize something, often subtly or without drawing attention. Can also imply being aware of something others might miss.

> "What, you thought I wasn't gon peep that?"

(See also: Peep Game)

Peep Game

/peep gaym/
(verb phrase)

To pay close attention to the underlying details or nuances of what's being said or done. It calls for heightened awareness and careful observation, encouraging someone to be discerning, and notice subtleties that might not be immediately obvious.

> *"Peep game, lil bruh, I'ma show you how to move."*

(See also: Peep)

Perpetrate

/pur-puh-trayt/
(verb)

To act in a way that misrepresents one's true character, status, or intentions; often used to describe someone putting on a false image to impress or deceive.

> *Frequently abbreviated as "perpin'."*
>
> *"She out here perpetrating like she got it like that."*

(See also: Lie To Kick It, Perpetrator, Play The Role)

Perpetrator

/pur-puh-tray-tor/
(noun)

Someone who pretends to be something they're not; often used to describe a person putting on a fake image or false persona.

> *"He don't even live like that for real, he just a perpetrator."*

(See also: Lie To Kick It, Perpetrate, Play The Role)

Pervin'

/pur-vin/
(noun)

Feeling the effects of alcohol, typically to the point of being drunk.

> "We was pervin' last night."

Pickle

/pik-uhl/
(noun)

A pound, typically of marijuana. Used in street and trade contexts to reference bulk weight without drawing attention.

> "They ran through that thang on the late night; got that boy for twenty-six pickles."

Pieces

/pee-siz/
(noun)

Jewelry, typically referring to noticeable or valuable items like chains, rings, bracelets, or watches.

> "He pulled up with all his pieces on, straight shinin'."

Pimp This Ol' S***

/pimp dis ohl s***/
(verb phrase)

To handle a difficult or high-pressure situation with confidence and calm authority. Suggests a refusal to succumb to adversity, rising to the occasion, and mastering the moment.

> "Everythang ain't perfect, but now, I'm finsta pimp this ol' s***."

Play The Role

/play thuh rohl/
(verb phrase)

To deliberately act or present oneself in a false manner, often to gain someone's trust or achieve a specific goal, typically while concealing one's true intentions.

> "She was just playin' the role until she got what she wanted."

(See also: Lie To Kick It, Perpetrate, Perpetrator)

PLAYER

A gentleman of elevated conduct with impeccable game; intellectual, charismatic, and emotionally composed. Potentially involved with multiple women, though typically with character than conquest. Not necessarily active in the game, but frequently mistaken to be, due to his energy, mindset, and demeanor.

Historically associated with the pimping profession as a traditional identifier, and often the preferred term over pimp, especially among older participants. Often used adjectively to describe behavior or style that reflects class, generosity, or refined taste.

Playerism is a philosophy. A player moves with intention, speaks with clarity, and carries himself with a quiet confidence that commands respect without demanding it.

> *The player archetype gained cultural momentum through the influence of Oakland's pimp culture in the 1970s, most notably through the 1973 film The Mack, filmed in Oakland. The movie helped codify the player's image: sharp, cool, and smooth. Too Short picked up where The Mack left off, embedding playerism into hip-hop's DNA.*

But beyond charisma, the true player is defined by his conduct, treating others with fairness, generosity, and respect. To be called a player is a compliment of the highest order. It speaks to one's character. A player keeps his word, honors his commitments, and carries himself with dignity. Rather than chase validation, he earns it through conviction and consistency. Sincerity is his credential.

The term has evolved over time, and today it's often used adjectively: *That was hella player of you* might describe a generous gesture, a classy move, or simply good form. In this sense, player becomes less about the women and more about the way.

Player Hate

/play-er hayt/
(verb)

To intentionally undermine, discredit, or block someone's success, confidence, or reputation, usually for selfish reasons such as jealousy, competition, or resentment. Player hating often involves talking down on someone, gossiping, throwing shade, or spreading misinformation in a way that does not serve a constructive purpose.

> *Expressing an opinion or valid criticism does not constitute player hating unless it is driven by envy or the desire to hinder someone. It strictly refers to actions meant to negatively impact someone out of personal bias or insecurity.*
>
> "They only player hate because they can't do what I do."

(See also: Hater, Player, Player Hater)

Player Price

/play-er pryce/
(phrase)

A discounted price or special deal, often offered as a favor or out of respect.

> "Bruh gave me the player price on the kicks."

(See also: Hooked, Joog)

PLAYER HATER

Someone who engages in player hating, actively seeking to undermine or diminish another person's success, reputation, or confidence, often out of jealousy, resentment, competition, or personal insecurity. This can involve obstructing opportunities, creating obstacles, spreading negativity or gossip, or downplaying achievements, particularly to elevate oneself at another's expense.

> *Motive and intent are key. Not all negative speech qualifies as player hating. Constructive criticism, personal opinions, and factual observations do not fall under this term unless they are driven by malicious intent.*

A player hater isn't simply someone who disagrees with you or challenges your ideas, rather someone who moves against you out of envy or spite, and often without justification.

The concept of the player hater emerged as the antithesis of the player. Where the player represents everything admirable: confidence, charisma, success, style, and integrity, the player hater represents the opposite.

> *Believed to have first appeared on record with Filthy Phil's 1990 "Player Haters" (Richmond, CA), though Poohman's 1992 Oakland release brought wider recognition. 2Pac affiliate The Gov also released "Player Hater" the same year.*

In The Bay, calling someone a player hater is a serious accusation. It suggests that their negativity stems not from legitimate concern but from a fundamental inability to celebrate someone else's wins.

The term is the precursor to the now more commonly used *hater,* an abbreviated form of *player hater* that has spread far beyond the Bay, becoming part of the mainstream American lexicon. The full phrase carried more weight, as a specific indictment of those who violated the unspoken code of respect that governs social interaction.

Playin' Wit Your Nose
/play-in wich-uh noz/
(phrase)

Snorting cocaine or having a habit of doing so; a discreet way of referring to cocaine use.

> "Bruh been playin' wit his nose heavy lately."

(See also: Nose Job, Pae Pae, Powda, Treat Your Nose)

Please Believe It
/pleez buh-leev it/
(expression)

Used to strongly confirm a statement or outcome as true, guaranteed, or inevitable. Carries the weight of absolutely, without question, or with the utmost certainty.

> "We goin' straight to the top if you not afraid; please believe it."

Plug
/pluhg/
(noun)

A reliable or advantageous source, often for drugs, deals, or hard-to-get items. May refer to a supplier, a small wholesale amount of drugs sold cheap enough to resell at a profit, or a connection to people, resources, or opportunities. Can also describe an unexpected discount or favorable hookup.

> "I needed 4 new tires; they plugged me for half off."

(See also: Hooked, Joog)

Po Po

/poh poh/
(noun)

The police.

> *A reduplication of "police."*
>
> *"Slow down, I think I seen the po po back there."*

(See also: 5-O, The Boys, The Rollers)

Pocket Watchin'

/pah-kit wotch-in/
(verb)

Being overly concerned with or monitoring someone else's financial situation or spending habits.

> *"Bruh always pocket watchin' instead of gettin' his own."*

(See also: Hatin')

Pockets Touchin'

/pah-kits tuh-chin/
(adjective)

Broke or out of money; having little to no cash on hand. The phrase paints a vivid image of empty pockets pressed together from lack of contents.

> *"I would slide, but my pockets touchin' right now, blud."*

(See also: Financially Embarrassed, Off)

Polar Bear

/poh-ler bair/
(noun)

A person from North Oakland, referencing the neighborhood's nickname, "The North Pole."

> References "The North Pole," a nickname for North Oakland.
>
> "He a polar bear, been reppin' the north his whole life."

(See also: The North Pole)

Poodle

/poo-dul/
(noun)

A coward, weakling, or someone seen as lacking toughness, resilience, or the ability to hold their own.

> "He act hard, but he really a poodle."

(See also: Busta, Mark, Noodle, Sucka, Weenie)

Pop

/pop/
(verb)

To approach someone with romantic intent, often in a bold or flirtatious way. Can also refer to shooting someone with a firearm.

> "I'ma pop at her when she get off work."
>
> "He got popped outside the store."

(See also: Get At, Holla, Spit Game)

Pop Your Collar

/pop ya kah-lah/
(verb phrase)

The act of literally tugging one's shirt collar upwards, or metaphorically adopting an attitude of confidence and pride. This gesture, whether physical or figurative, is used to celebrate personal achievements and convey a sense of self-assuredness and grandeur.

> *"He just closed that deal, let him pop his collar."*

(See also: Collar Pop, Collar Popper, Collar Poppin')

Poppin' The Most

/pop-in thuh mohst/
(phrase)

1980s slang for "excellent" or "the best."

> *"We seniors this year, straight poppin' the most."*

Posted

/poh-stid/
(adjective, verb)

Remaining in one place, often for a long period. In street contexts, it may also suggest holding down a spot, especially in relation to territorial presence or illegal activity such as drug sales.

> *"We was posted on the block all night."*

Potna

/pot-nuh/
(noun)

A close friend or associate; commonly used in the Bay Area, especially Oakland. While often a term of camaraderie similar to bra or blud, it can carry a more serious or even aggressive tone depending on the context.

> Phonetic spelling of "partner," reflecting regional pronunciation.
>
> "That's my potna, we go way back."
>
> "You better chill out, potna, before it go left."

(See also: Cuddie, Folks, Rogue)

Pound

/pown/
(noun, verb)

Describes deep, heavy bass played at high volume. Can refer to the act of blasting bass or the presence and intensity of the sound itself.

> "That old school was poundin' down the block."

(See also: Bump, Knock, Slap, Subin')

Pow Wow

/pow wow/
(noun)

A playful or shortened form of powda, referring to cocaine in its powdered form, as opposed to crack or rock cocaine.

> "They was up all night goin' dumb off that pow wow."

(See also: Pae Pae, Powda)

Powda

/pow-duh/
(noun)

Cocaine in its powdered form, distinguishing it from crack or rock cocaine.

> *Phonetic spelling of "powder."*
>
> *"He started off just smokin' weed, now he done graduated to powda."*

(See also: Pae Pae, Pow Wow)

Powderhead

/pow-der-hed/
(noun)

A cocaine addict, specifically someone who uses cocaine in its powdered form, as opposed to crack.

> *"He snortin' up her whole check. That boi a straight powderhead."*

(See also: Playin' Wit Your Nose)

Pull Up

/pul uhp/
(verb phrase)

To arrive or stop by, usually in a vehicle.

> *"Ya'll on the block? I'm finna pull up."*

(See also: Yank Up)

Pump Fakin'

/puhmp fay-kin/
(verb)

The act of leading someone to believe you will take a certain action, only to not follow through, often after showing initial signs of commitment.

> From basketball, where a player fakes a shot to deceive the defender.
>
> "She tap in every couple weeks, actin' like she ready. She pump fakin' tho."

Pump Fear

/puhmp feer/
(verb phrase)

To attempt to intimidate someone using threats or aggressive talk, often without backing it up with real action.

> "He wasn't really tryna fight, just tryna pump fear."

Punk Rock

/puhngk rahk/
(noun)

A derogatory term for a woman of low character, typically one who acts without morals, self-respect, or accountability. Often refers to someone willing to lie, cheat, steal, or manipulate others without regard for consequences, fairness, or integrity. Commonly used to express strong disapproval when a woman's behavior is viewed as deplorable or completely unacceptable.

> *Often shortened to "punk" in casual usage.*
>
> *"She lied the whole time, and acted like she did nothing wrong. Straight punk rock."*

(See also: Faggit)

Purple

/pur-pul/
(noun)

A potent strain of marijuana known for its distinctive purple hairs or coloration.

> *Sometimes shortened to "purp."*
>
> *"Bruh rolled up some fire purple last night."*

(See also: Dank, Gas, Grapes)

Push A (Hard) Line

/puhsh uh hard lyn/
(phrase)

To uncompromisingly advocate or adhere to a particular stance or approach, often with strong conviction and without yielding.

> "I get that this your spot, but now, you pushin' a hard line."

Put In Check

/put in chek/
(phrase)

A phrase related to check, used to describe a stern or scolding correction that puts someone in their place, akin to restricting a piece's movement in chess. This term often leads to shame or embarrassment for the corrected party, emphasizing a forceful and often public assertion of authority.

> "She musta forgot who she was talkin' to, I had to put her in check one time."

Put It On Thick

/put it awn thik/
(verb phrase)

To exaggerate or overemphasize, often to deceive or impress.

> "You told me baby was cute. You put that on extra thick."

(See also: 2 On The 10, Lie To Kick It)

Put On Blast

/put awn blast/
(verb phrase)

To expose or call someone out publicly, often revealing personal, embarrassing, or incriminating information.

> *"She really put him on blast talkin' 'bout he still live with his moms."*

(See also: Clown, Front Street, Fronted Off)

Quarter Spoon

/kwor-dur spoon/
(noun)

A term for a quarter of a million dollars ($250,000).

> "Bruh hit a tremendous lick. Came up on a quarter spoon."

Quo Vadis

/kwo vah-dis/
(noun)

A Louieville-style haircut with no defined line, worn low and even all around. Often regarded as an unfashionable or outdated cut, typically associated with strict parents or those unaware of current trends.

> *The name, borrowed from the 1951 film Quo Vadis, may subtly allude to Roman-inspired styles, similar to the East Coast "Caesar" cut.*

> "He came through with the Quo Vadis, hella low, no line. Moms must've picked it."

(See also: Louisville)

Rack

/rak/
(noun)

One thousand dollars.

"Blud owe me a rack, I ain't seen him in six weeks."

(See also: Band, Thou-Wow)

Rathead

/rat-hed/
(noun)

A woman who embodies or subscribes to the worst aspects of ghetto culture.

An alternative form of "hoodrat."

Often abbreviated to "rat," which has become the more commonly used form.

"She be loud, messy, and always in drama; straight rat."

Raw

/raw/
(adjective)

Used to describe someone who is exceptionally good, talented, or skillful, especially in sports, music, or performance. Can also refer to sexual activity without the use of protection.

> "Back in the day I seen J. Kidd go for 40 in a high school game. Blud was hella raw."
>
> "You don't know baby like that to be goin' raw. You might wanna use some protection, bro."

(See also: Clean, Raw Dog, Run Raw, Saucy)

Raw Dog

/raw dawg/
(verb)

To engage in sexual intercourse without protection.

> Sometimes alternatively spelled "raw dawg."
>
> "Bruh really tried to raw dawg off the first link."

(See also: Raw, Run Raw)

Real Talk
/reel tawk/
(phrase)

A declaration used to emphasize that the speaker is being honest, sincere, or straightforward. It signals that the following or preceding statement is made without exaggeration, deceit, or irony, often used to underscore the seriousness or importance of the conversation.

> "I think you should reconsider that move you 'bout to make, real talk."

Reckless
/rek-lis/
(adjective)

Describes a woman who engages in excessive, suggestive, or inappropriate eye contact with another man, despite being in a relationship. Often refers to stepping out of line through flirtation or visible interest that disrespects her current relationship.

> *A truncation of "reckless eye-ballin'," a term rooted in pimp culture.*
>
> "She got a man but still over there bein' reckless."

Reptable

/rep-tuh-bull/
(noun, adjective)

A person respected, or held in high regard, typically well-known and in good community standing; also used to describe behavior or conduct expected of someone with that level of reputation.

> *A twist on "reputable," formed through mispronunciation and reinterpretation, retaining its sense of respect while emphasizing social standing and expected conduct.*
>
> *"Bruh been solid for years, everybody know he a reptable."*
>
> *"Nah, you can't move like that, that's not reptable behavior."*

(See also: Factor, Major Factor)

Rest Haven

/rest hay-vin/
(noun)

A man who provides refuge or shelter to a woman from her former relationship, allowing her to escape previous restrictions or responsibilities. It implies that her new environment is more lenient, with fewer demands, expectations, or boundaries.

> *Derived from pimp culture.*
>
> *"She blew up on bra pretty quick. He was just a rest haven."*

Reverse Game

/rih-vurs gaym/
(verb phrase)

To turn the tables on someone, especially by outsmarting or undermining them using their own tactics or position against them.

> "He tried to pull a slick move, but I had to reverse game."

The Rich

/thuh rich/
(noun)

Richmond, California.

> Often referred to as "Rich City."
>
> "Lil Mama kinda different. You know she from The Rich."

Ripper

/rip-er/
(noun)

A promiscuous woman.

> Possibly originated as a phonetic alteration of "stripper."
>
> "She fasho a ripper, messin' with the whole crew."

(See also: Runner)

Ripper Slippers

/rip-uh slip-uhz/
(noun)

Plastic mesh house slippers known for being inexpensive and lightweight. Commonly associated with lower-income urban fashion in the Bay Area.

> "She out here in pajama pants and ripper slippers again."

(See also: Ripper)

Roasted

/roh-stid/
(adjective)

To be made fun of or insulted, often in a playful or mocking manner.

> "He got roasted by his friends for his new haircut."

(See also: Capped On, Clown, Whoride)

Rockin'

/rahk-in/
(verb)

Reflects both how someone carries themselves, including their stance, mindset, or way of handling situations, and what they choose to accept, support, or participate in.

> "They tried to get me to do something bootsie, I told 'em I wasn't even rockin' like that."

(See also: Get Down)

Rogue
/rohg/
(noun)

A term similar to bro, bruh, folks, or potna, used exclusively in the East Palo Alto (E.P.A.) and Menlo Park regions to refer to a friend or acquaintance.

> "What's up rogue, how you feelin' today?"

Rolled Up
/rohld up/
(verb)

Caught; found out.

> "I almost got away wit it, but I got rolled up at the last minute."

The Rollers
/thuh roh-lerz/
(noun)

The police.

> "Slow down, bro, there go the rollers."

(See also: 5-O, The Boys, Po Po)

Rollin'

/roh-lin/
(adjective)

Experiencing a high volume of activity, business, or sales; consistently busy or thriving.

> "The barbershop was rollin' on Saturday."

Run Mine

/run myn/
(verb phrase)

A direct demand for something owed or rightfully belonging to the speaker, often delivered with urgency or assertiveness.

> "You got my money, breh? Run mine."

(See also: Break Bread, Cash Me Out, Kick Me Down)

Run Raw

/run raw/
(verb phrase)

To have unprotected sex.

> "She tried to get me to run raw after about two months."

(See also: Raw, Raw Dog)

Run Up

/run up/
(verb phrase)

To approach someone aggressively, often with the intent to confront or initiate a conflict.

> "Run up and see what happen."

Runner

/run-er/
(noun)

A woman perceived as promiscuous or known for having multiple sexual partners, often simultaneously.

> The abbreviated form "run" can also refer to such a woman, or function as a verb meaning to engage in sex with a woman, often used casually or disrespectfully.
>
> "Don't wife her bra, she a cold runner."

(See also: Bopper, Ripper, Toss Up)

Runnin'

/ruhn-in/
(adjective)

Used to describe a car that's fast, often with strong acceleration.

> "You don't wanna race bruh Camaro, that thang runnin'."

S.F.C.

/ess-eff-see/
(initialism, noun)

An initialism for "San Francisco", California.

Also used locally to mean "Sucka Free City," a cultural nickname that conveys regional pride while rejecting "sucka" behavior.

"I was born and raised in that S.F.C. mayne, the Sucka Free City."

(See also: The City, E.P.A., E.S.O., Frisco, San Fran)

Sack

/sak/
(noun)

A bag of drugs.

"I heard he got the sack."

Salibone

/sal-ee-bohn/
(noun)

A childhood prank involving a playful but often stinging slap to the back of the neck, delivered by surprise, usually by a friend, while yelling "Salibone!" at the moment of contact. It's meant to be more humorous than harmful.

"I was walkin' by and bruh hit me with a salibone outta nowhere."

Salt Your Game

/sawlt yer gaym/
(phrase)

Describes the act of intentionally undermining or sabotaging someone's efforts in social or romantic pursuits, often due to jealousy or rivalry.

> *Sometimes stylized as "throwing salt," or "threw salt on my game."*
>
> *"Don't salt my game by telling her those stories about me."*

(See also: Player Hate, Salted Out)

Salted Out

/sawlt-id owt/
(phrase)

Describes a situation where someone, typically a rival or jealous person, negatively influences a potential love interest's perception of you, effectively sabotaging your romantic chances.

> *"Baby was ready to bite, then I got salted out."*

(See also: Player Hate, Salt Your Game)

San Fran

/san fran/
(noun)

An abbreviated name for San Francisco, often signaling that the speaker is new to or not native to the Bay Area.

> *Rarely, if ever, used by Bay Area locals, who prefer the terms "Frisco" or "The City."*
>
> *"He kept callin' it San Fran, so I knew he wasn't from out here."*

(See also: The City, Frisco)

Saucy

/saw-see/
(adjective)

Something or someone that is stylish or impressive.

> *"They just dropped that new Corvette, that thang hella saucy."*

(See also: Clean, Wet)

Sav

/sav/
(adjective)

An abbreviated form of savage, used to describe someone who is bold, daring, or fearless. It often implies a readiness to take action without hesitation, whether in physical confrontations, social situations, or high-pressure environments. While typically positive, the term can also suggest recklessness depending on context. To a lesser extent, it can carry connotations of courage or audacity.

> *"Lil bro ain't scared of nothin', he a real sav."*

Sav It Out

/sav it owt/
(verb phrase)

To face a tough or high-pressure situation with boldness, fearlessness, and determination; combines endurance with audacity, often implying doing whatever it takes without backing down.

> *Similar to "thug it out," but with a stronger emphasis on daring and fearless action.*
>
> *"It got ugly for a minute, but I had to sav it out and handle my business."*

(See also: Boss Up, Sav, Thug It Out)

Savin'

/say-vin/
(verb)

Intervening on behalf of a woman in an excessive or unnecessary way, typically to gain her favor or approval.

> *The term is closely associated with, and likely derived from, Captain Save-A-Hoe.*
>
> *"Bruh stay savin' baby, she don't even fool with him like that."*

(See also: Captain)

Scary

/skair-ee/
(adjective)

Used to describe someone who is easily frightened, avoids confrontation, or lacks courage. Often said dismissively to suggest the person poses no real threat.

> "You ain't gotta worry about blud, he hella scary."

(See also: Mark, Noodle, Poodle, Sucka)

Scoop

/skoop/
(verb)

To come and pick someone up, usually in a car. Emphasizes the act of pulling up to collect someone, rather than giving them a ride.

> "You off work yet? I'ma come scoop you."

(See also: Snatch, Swoop)

Scrape

/skrayp/
(verb)

To decisively defeat or overcome someone, typically in a competitive or confrontational situation. Can also refer to driving a scraper, a type of modified car associated with Bay Area culture.

> "The Warriors got scraped by Dub last night."

> "I just seen bra scrape by with the whistle tip and the speakers in the grill."

(See also: Molly Whopped, Mopped)

Scraper

/skray-per/
(noun)

A term from Bay Area car culture describing an older car, often a 1990s era Buick, that is modified with features like large rims. These vehicles are typically customized with modifications such as whistle tips, loud stereo systems, speakers in the grill, large chrome rims, TV monitors in the headrests, and custom paint jobs.

> *Common scraper models include Buick Park Avenue, Buick Regal, Buick LeSabre, Pontiac Bonneville, Buick Century, Buick Reatta, Oldsmobile Cutlass Ciera, Pontiac Grand Prix, Lexus SC, and others.*
>
> *"He bought the scraper wit the tv's already in the headrest."*

(See also: The Hyphy Movement)

Scraper Bike

/skray-per byk/
(noun)

A type of customized bicycle popular in Bay Area street culture, characterized by brightly colored frames, oversized rims, and often adorned with eye-catching decorations. *Scraper bikes* are typically modified by their owners to mimic the style of *scraper cars*, including elements like foil, tape, and painted spokes.

> *"The scraper bikes was out deep at First Friday."*

(See also: Scraper)

Scrub

/skruhb/
(verb/noun)

To fall hard, often while running or moving fast. As a noun, also refers to a weak link, or unskilled player on a sports team.

> The term likely comes from the idea of "scrubbing" the ground with your body during the fall.
>
> "Bruh was runnin' full speed and scrubbed hella hard."
>
> "Coach need a 20 point cushion before he put the scrubs in."

(See also: Bap)

See Me

/see mee/
(verb phrase)

A challenge to fight; a way of telling someone to meet you physically if they have a problem.

> "Keep talkin' slick, you gon have to see me."

(See also: Chunk 'Em, Get Em Up)

Sellin'

/sel-in/
(verb)

Describes the compromising of one's values, dignity, integrity, or authenticity, often for personal gain, acceptance, or approval. It carries a strong negative connotation, implying betrayal of self or community principles for superficial rewards. Commonly understood as a shortened form of phrases like selling out or selling your soul. Sometimes used among friends to call out someone who is being manipulated or trying too hard, particularly where romantic interests are concerned.

> *"You tryin' hella hard to impress that lil broad, huh? You sellin', breh."*

(See also: Go Out)

Servin'

/sir-vin/
(verb)

To skillfully maneuver a car, whipping, spinning, or sliding to draw attention and showcase control, often pushing the vehicle to its fullest potential. Can also refer to convincingly defeating or overwhelming someone, especially in a competitive setting; or, in another context, to dealing or handing out drugs.

> *"He on the block servin' straight love."*

(See also: Dosin', Grinding, Swang)

Sewed

/sohd/
(verb)

A situation, outcome, or person that is under complete control or fully secured. Implies confidence, certainty, or dominance in a given scenario.

> "Don't even trip, I got it sewed."

Shag

/shag/
(noun)

A haircut characterized by shorter length on the top and sides, with longer hair in the back or neck area.

> "He still rockin' that old school shag."

Shake The Spot

/shayk thuh spaht/
(verb phrase)

To leave or depart from a location.

> "It got a lil too hyphy, so we had to shake the spot."

(See also: Bounce, Cut, Dip, Do It Movin', Slide)

Shoobie Doobie
/shoo-bee doo-bee/
(noun)

A flirtatious term for a young woman thought to be single, attractive, or desirable; typically delivered in a playful, or charismatic manner.

> *Derived from pimp culture.*
>
> *"Look at lil mama across the street; that's a nice lil shoobie doobie right there."*

Shoot Dice
/shoot dys/
(verb phrase)

To play the traditional street version of craps using two dice, typically for money and often with fast-paced action and neighborhood rules.

> *In the Bay Area, the phrase "shoot dice" is uniquely preferred over alternatives like "play dice," "shoot/roll craps," or games like cee-lo (which uses three dice), all of which may reveal someone as being from outside the region.*
>
> *"We was on Seminary hella deep, shootin' dice."*

Short Stop
/shoht stahp/
(verb)

To intercept business or customers intended for someone else, usually by inserting yourself between a competitor and their source of traffic. Often used in street-level drug dealing, where a dealer sets up between the competition and their customer base, effectively taking their sales.

> "He out there short stoppin', catching all the knocks before they come upstairs."

Shot To The Curb
/shaht tuh thuh kerb/
(phrase)

Extremely unattractive, worn out, or damaged, often to the point of needing replacement. Also a way to describe being romantically rejected or dismissed.

> Commonly shortened to "shot."
>
> "I tried to holla at her, but she shot me to the curb."
>
> "You need to throw them kicks in the garbage, them thangs shot to the curb."

(See also: Thru)

Sic

/sik/
(adjective)

A term for someone seen as either dangerously aggressive or exceptionally gifted. It can also stretch to describe actions that cross a line into questionable or outrageous. The tone can swing from admiration to criticism depending on context.

> "Don't get on bruh bad side, that boi sic."
>
> "Bruh can really rap, that boi sic on the mic."
>
> "You messin' with her? You a sic dude."

Side

/syd/
(verb)

To act with an air of superiority, either by dismissing or ignoring someone, or by confidently displaying possessions or style to impress others.

> *Possibly derived from "highside" or "side bust," or as a blended form of both.*
>
> "I've known her for years, I can't believe she tried to side on me like that."
>
> "They came through the ave in the drop 'Stang on thangs, straight sidin'."

Side Bust

/syd bust/
(verb)

To flaunt one's possessions or achievements in a manner that highlights the disparity between oneself and those with less. Often used to describe behavior that is perceived as showing off at the expense of others.

> "That's yo problem bra, you always tryin' to side bust."

(See also: Highside, Side, Side Buster)

Side Buster

/syd bust-er/
(noun)

Someone who flaunts their advantages, often in a way that demeans or overshadows those with less.

> The term may have influenced the later use of the word "busta."
>
> "Even when he wear a collared shirt, he force his chain over it. He a true side buster."

(See also: Busta, Flossin', Highside)

SIDESHOW

An informal street gathering originating in Oakland, California, where people congregate to showcase vehicles, status, and style, with a backdrop of music and socializing.

Fueled by the prosperity of the local drug trade and a broader economic boom, the sideshows of the 1980s through the early 2000s were initially associated with high-end classic cars and participants with wealth, also displaying jewelry, outfits, and other markers of success.

Over time, they evolved to focus more on car stunts and disorderly conduct, reflecting broader changes in the community and its economic conditions.

> *The 1990 song "Sideshow" by Oakland rapper Richie Rich (of 415) documents the early era of the event, emphasizing the social and material showcase aspects of the gatherings before they shifted toward car stunts and disorderly conduct.*

Sideways

/side-wayz/
(adverb)

A term used to describe the action of a car, motorcycle, or other vehicle when the rear end swings out and "fishtails" during acceleration, causing it to move forward at an angle. Often associated with high-performance muscle cars, this motion represents power, speed, and control. The term also extends to mean leaving quickly, evoking the image of peeling out from a stoplight. The term is also used to describe behavior that is disrespectful, hostile, or confrontational. In such expressions, it functions within verb phrases to convey action or stance.

> "He hit the corner sideways in the '72 Cutlass."
> "Y'all could stay if y'all want to, I'm sideways."
> "You comin' at me sideways tho, bra."

Skantless

/skan(t)-liss/
(adjective)

Describes behavior that is selfish, heartless, or morally wrong, often involving betrayal, disloyalty, or a lack of integrity.

> *Intentional variation of "scandalous," often pronounced "scan-less."*
> "He left her right after she had the baby; hella skantless."

Skrilla

/skril-uh/
(noun)

A term used to refer to money.

> *Often shortened to "skrill."*
>
> *"He out here stackin' skrilla like it's nothin'."*

(See also: Bank, Mail, Paper)

Slap

/slap/
(noun, verb)

A term for music that is considered exceptionally good, often used to describe songs, albums, or car sound systems that deliver loud, high-quality audio, often characterized by heavy bass. It can also refer to the act of playing or listening to such music. Additionally, slap functions as a cross-functional idiom meaning to put something on or apply it with ease or emphasis, often referring to upgrades, additions, or details. In musical contexts, this phrasing may simply mean to play a song or album.

> *"That old school Chevy had hella slap in the trunk."*
>
> *"Slap that Mess again."*
>
> *"I just slapped some gold thangs on the Chev."*
>
> *"This beat slap hella hard."*

(See also: Beat, Blap, Bump, Knock)

Slapper

/slap-er/
(noun)

A song that is particularly enjoyable and well-regarded, primarily for its compelling beat.

> "Play that last track again, breh, that was a slapper."

Slide

/slahyd/
(verb)

A versatile term used to describe smooth or deliberate action across various contexts. It can mean visiting or leaving a place, confronting someone with intent to retaliate, having sex, performing impressively on a music track, using a fraudulent card, or handing something off as a favor.

> "What you doin? I'm 'bout to slide through."
>
> "They about to go slide on them boys about that disrespect."
>
> "How you like my new shoes? I slid for these."
>
> "We supposed to kick it again tonight; hopefully she let me slide."
>
> "He really slid on that track, like he murdered the beat."

Slider

/sly-der/
(noun)

A fraudulent credit or gift card used in illegal transactions.

> "That slider bra had was hittin', he came up."

Slippin'
/slip-in/
(verb)

Negligence or inattentiveness that may lead to adverse circumstances or situations.

> "Yo wallet was on the bathroom floor bra, you slippin'."

(See also: Caught Slippin')

Slump
/sluhmp/
(noun, verb)

A fusion of the terms slap and bump, used to describe music with deep bass and heavy impact. Can refer to the sound itself or the act of playing it.

> "They slid through in the glass house slumpin' hella hard."

(See also: Bump, Knock, Slap, Tremendo)

Slumped
/sluhmpt/
(verb)

Murdered; shot and killed.

> "Bra got slumped last night."

(See also: Downt, Knocked Down, Laminated, Smacked, Smoked)

Slumper

/sluhm-per/
(noun)

A song with deep bass and strong low-end presence that is also musically appealing. Commonly used to describe tracks that combine bass-heavy production with an enjoyable or satisfying sound.

> "This one a real slumper."

(See also: Slapper, Slump)

Slunder

/sluhn-der/
(noun)

A phonetic alteration of "under," used with the same meaning to describe low-key or inconspicuous behavior.

> "Bruh been on the slunder since the funk popped off."

(See also: Under)

Smacked

/smakt/
(verb)

Shot and killed, typically in the context of a targeted or intentional act. Also used to describe suffering a heavy financial loss, especially in gambling or hustling situations.

> "You heard what happened? Bra got smacked last night."
>
> "I got smacked at the dice game last night and left broke."

(See also: Downt, Hit, Knocked Down, Struck, Stung)

Smackin'

/smack-in/
(adjective)

Food that is exceptionally tasty or delicious; often used to describe a meal that greatly exceeds expectations in flavor or satisfaction.

> *Sometimes pronounced "shmackin'."*
> "That BBQ plate was smackin'."

Small Thing To A Giant

/smahl thayng tuh uh jy-uhnt/
(phrase)

Used to downplay the difficulty or importance of a task, challenge, or situation, framing it as minor in comparison to one's ability, stature, or experience. Often said with calm confidence to suggest ease, control, or resilience.

> "Bruh tried to throw salt on my game, but I ain't trippin'. It's a small thing to a giant."

(See also: Balloons To A Blimp, Peanuts To An Elephant)

Smash

/smash/
(verb)

To act with aggressive force or urgency. Commonly refers to bullying, intimidation, or harsh verbal scolding; taking something by force or acting greedily, like cutting in line or overindulging. The term is also used to describe driving at high speeds, often recklessly or with urgency.

> *Variants include "smashin'" (ongoing action) and "smash on" (emphasizing direct confrontation).*
>
> *"They finna close, but if you smash you could make it."*
>
> *"He kept talkin' slick, so I had to smash on him."*
>
> *"They smashed on the snacks before anybody else got some."*

(See also: Mobbin')

Smash Artist

/smash ahr-tist/
(noun)

A person known for acting with force, urgency, or assertiveness in various situations, often in a way that is excessive or opportunistic. The term is frequently used in a joking or offhand manner to describe someone's bold, audacious, or greedy behavior.

> *"She hopped in the fifteen-items-or-less line wit about a hunnid things. She a cold smash artist."*

(See also: Smash, Smash Tactics)

Smash Tactics

/smash tak-tiks/
(noun)

The specific methods someone uses to intimidate, dominate, or pressure others through aggressive or uncompromising behavior, frequently by leveraging a position of power, advantage, or influence.

> "Oh, I see how you movin', you tryin' to use smash tactics."

(See also: Smash, Smash Artist)

Smirkish

/smurk-ish/
(adjective)

Used to describe someone who seems sneaky or devious, like they're always plotting, hiding something, or can't fully be trusted. The term draws from the kind of smirk someone might wear when they know something you don't or are up to no good.

> "I don't trust bruh like that, he too smirkish for me."

Smobbin'

/smaw-bin/
(verb)

A phonetic variation of "mobbin'," used with the same meaning. Refers to driving fast, aggressively, or confidently, often in a familiar area or street setting. May also describe moving with purpose or intensity, either alone, or as a group.

> Believed to be a blend of "smashin'" and "mobbin'."
>
> "We was smobbin' through the East last night."

(See also: Mobbin')

Smoked

/smohkt/
(verb)

To be shot and killed, or becoming extremely high from marijuana.

> "They smoked him in broad daylight."
>
> "We hit that new strain and got smoked."

(See also: Downt, Knocked Down, Laminated, Slumped, Smacked)

Snatch

/snach/
(verb)

To pick up or collect someone in a vehicle, to buy or obtain something, or to persuade someone's love interest away from them.

> "I'm about to go snatch her from work real quick."
>
> "I might have to go snatch them blue Pradas."
>
> "Dude think he got her sewed up, but I think I could snatch."

So Quick, So Fast
/soh kwik soh fast/
(phrase)

An emphatic affirmation or punctuation to a statement of certainty, suggesting something will happen immediately, without delay, and beyond question. Often used alongside phrases like off top or please believe it to reinforce confidence and inevitability.

> "We does the damn thang, all day every day, off top, on my momma, so quick and so fast, please believe it."

(See also: Fasho, Off Top, On Citas, On Mommas, Please Believe It)

Soak Game
/sohk gaym/
(verb phrase)

To listen, observe, and take in valuable knowledge or insight, especially from those who are more experienced or skilled. Often used in contexts where someone is learning the social, romantic, street, or entrepreneurial principles known as game. The phrase suggests paying close attention in order to increase one's understanding or ability.

> "Stop talkin' and soak game when the real ones speak."

(See also: Game, Peep Game)

Soft

/sawft/
(adjective, noun)

Typically used to refer to money that falls just short of its full measure. Also refers to powder cocaine in contrast to "hard" (crack or rock cocaine).

> "Bruh said he paid a soft band for the rims, like $973."
> "However you want it, he got it hard or soft."

Solid

/sah-lid/
(adjective)

Dependable, trustworthy, and showing strong integrity, either as a personal quality or through an action that reflects those values.

> "Bruh solid, always comes through when you need him."
> "They wanted him to snitch, but he kept it solid."

Spin Off

/spin-awf/
(verb phrase)

To leave or walk away, often with swift or intentional motion, reflecting the physical act of turning to exit.

> "She said what she had to say and spun off."

(See also: Bounce, Cut, Shake The Spot, Sideways)

Spit

/spit/
(verb)

To talk or converse, often in a smooth, persuasive, or confident manner. Frequently used in the context of rap lyrics or romantic interest.

> *"She over there starin' at you, go spit at her."*
>
> *"Bruh can really spit, he been rappin' since middle school."*

Spit Game

/spit gaym/
(verb phrase)

To speak or converse with eloquence and intelligence, skillfully using advanced vernacular to demonstrate understanding, connect concepts meaningfully, and express ideas with substance, wisdom, and insight. Often delivered with persuasive intent, whether flirtatiously to impress a love interest or intellectually to convey depth, insight, and command of language.

> *"I love hangin' wit unk, he be spittin' game."*

(See also: Mouthpiece)

Sport

/spohrt/
(verb)

To treat or cover the cost for someone, usually as an act of generosity or camaraderie; often used when one person helps another financially or looks out for them in a time of need.

> Often pronounced "spote."
>
> "I'm doin' bad, sport yo potna one time."

Sport Coat

/spote koht/
(noun, verb)

A man who caters to or provides for a woman in an excessive or undeserved way, often seen as naïve or lacking game. The term typically contrasts with a street-savvy man, portraying instead a lame or easily manipulated type. As a verb, sport coating refers to engaging in that behavior, covering the cost or "sporting" someone beyond reason or respect. The term implies misplaced generosity or weakness.

> *Thought to originate, or at least gain popular exposure, through 2Pac's 1996 song "Ratha Be Ya N****," featuring Richie Rich, whose lyric is believed to have potentially introduced the phrase.*
>
> *"He be perpetratin' like he a player, bra ain't nothin' but a ole sport coat."*

(See also: Captain, Savin', Sport)

Sprung

/spruhng/
(adjective)

Deeply infatuated, enamored, or captivated by someone, often to the point of losing composure or acting irrationally. Can refer to being head over heels in love, having a strong crush, or being enchanted by someone's presence, appearance, or attention.

> "Bruh only known her for two weeks and he already sprung."
>
> "You can tell she got that boy sprung the way he be actin'."

Spunky

/spuhn-kee/
(adjective)

Situations, environments, or individuals that are involved in or prone to conflict and aggressive actions.

> "What's hatnin' bra? I know you not tryin' to get spunky."

Squat

/skwot/
(verb)

To own or drive a particular car, often implying a sense of identity associated with the vehicle.

> The term comes from the way a vehicle's rear end dips downward when accelerating, creating a "squatting" motion.
>
> "I'm squattin' a little mobby for right now."

Stack
/stak/
(verb)

To save or accumulate money; also refers to the money saved, often in large or organized amounts.

> "I been stackin' all year."

The Stack
/thuh stak/
(noun)

A nickname for Hayward, California.

> "I had moved out there to The Stack for a couple years."

Static
/stat-ik/
(noun)

Tension, conflict, or trouble with someone.

> "He don't want no static with me."

Stay-Highs

/stay-hyz/
(noun)

A style of sunglasses characterized by small, rectangular tinted lenses, available in a variety of colors. Popular in the Bay Area during the late 1990s and early 2000s, the name Stay-Highs refers to the way the tint concealed the eyes, often used to hide redness or glossiness from smoking marijuana. Worn in a range of settings, including indoors or at night, reinforcing their association with a laid-back and low-key style.

> *"He slid through with some red Stay-Highs on."*

(See also: Stunnas)

Stayin' Out The Way

/stay-in owt thuh way/
(verb phrase)

Keeping a low profile and avoiding drama, trouble, or unnecessary involvement. Implies minding your business while letting others do their thing without interference. Often said in response to a question about one's well-being.

> *"I ain't been doin' too much, just stayin' out the way."*

Steady

/sted-ee/
(adverb)

Used to highlight persistent or ongoing behavior, whether positive or negative. Often emphasizes that someone keeps doing something without letting up.

> "You steady in my business."
>
> "He steady makin' plays."

Steppin' On S***

/step-in on s***/
(verb phrase)

Moving with aggression, dominance, and a no-mercy mindset; overcoming opposition, clearing out enemies, or seizing control of territory, resources, or respect. Often used to describe someone asserting power in the streets in a ruthless, uncompromising way. Can also apply to dominating in competitive settings like sports, business, or personal success.

> "Ever since he got out, bruh been steppin' on s***."

Stick To The Script

/stik tuh thuh skript/
(verb phrase)

To remain dedicated and committed to established rules, values, and expectations, whether spoken or unspoken. Often used to emphasize consistency, discipline, and not straying from agreed-upon standards or principles.

> "No matter what happen, bruh always stick to the script."

Stole On

/stohl awn/
(verb)

Refers to the act of punching someone, typically catching the person off guard.

> "He kept on bumpin' his gums 'til he got stole on."

Stolo

/stoh-loh/
(noun)

A stolen car.

> "They runnin' round hittin' licks in a stolo."

Straight

/strayt/
(adjective)

Affirming that someone or something is real, solid, or 100%. Often refers to authenticity, loyalty, or seriousness.

> "That's my straight folks."
>
> "He out here straight ballin'."

Straight Up

/strayt uhp/
(phrase)

Used to emphasize sincerity or truthfulness, often placed at the end of a sentence to confirm something genuinely or without exaggeration.

> "I told him I wasn't playin' no games, straight up."

Strike

/stryk/
(verb)

To drive or move quickly, often with urgency or purpose. Can also refer to traveling a long distance, typically by car.

> "You need a ride to Stockton? Damn, that's a strike."

(See also: Burl, Hully, Mobbin')

Strip

/strip/
(verb)

To rob someone of everything in their possession, often at gunpoint.

> *"He went down there flossin' all that jewelry and got stripped."*

The Strip

/thuh strip/
(noun)

The section of Foothill Blvd spanning from 73rd Ave to High St.

> *Also referred to more technically as "The Foothill Strip."*

> *While these boundaries are widely recognized, some consider The Strip to extend as far west as Lake Merritt and as far east as the Oakland/San Leandro border.*

> *"It was hella work on The Strip last night."*

Struck

/struhk/
(verb)

To lose or gain a significant amount of money, especially through gambling, betting, or games of chance. Context determines whether the outcome was positive or negative. Also serves as the past tense of strike, meaning to drive or move quickly, often with urgency or purpose.

> *"I got struck in the dice game last night."*

> *"I struck to the house to grab my wallet."*

(See also: Hit, Smacked, Stung)

Stuck

/stuhk/
(adjective)

Rendered speechless or physically unresponsive, often due to marijuana, other drug intoxication, fear, or overwhelming embarrassment. Also used to describe being left in a bad position or without options.

> *Sometimes phrased as "on stuck mode" or "left on stuck" in casual speech.*
>
> "Damn, boi. You over there stuck."
>
> "Bruh hit the blunt and been on stuck mode ever since."
>
> "Bruh said he was gon' help but never showed. Left me on stuck."

Stuey

/stoo-ee/
(adjective)

A stylized variation of "stupid," used with the same meaning to describe something noticeably impressive, or standout. Commonly applied to jewelry, cars, or outfits that appear extravagant or high-level, as well as events that are crowded, exciting, or memorable.

> *"We hit that new spot downtown last night. It was goin' stuey in that g-thang."*

(See also: Dumb, Off The Hook, Stupid)

Stung

/stuhng/
(verb)

To take a financial loss, often in a way that feels sharp or painful. Implies the sting of losing money, particularly in gambling, hustling, or risky situations.

> *"I tried to double up at the tables and got stung for a quick rack."*

(See also: Hit, Smacked, Struck)

Stunnas

/stuhn-uhz/
(noun)

A shortened form of Stunna Shades, referring to oversized or attention-grabbing sunglasses typically worn to make a bold impression. The style followed earlier Bay Area trends like *Stay-Highs* and aviator-style glasses popularized by brands such as Blue Blocker. Over time, larger lenses became the standard, with stunnas emerging as the defining term for bold, statement-making shades closely associated with stuntin' and visual self-expression. In older usage, stunnas has also referred to ecstasy pills, though this meaning is far less common.

> *"I just snatched some saucy stunnas at Durant."*

Stuntin'

/stuhn-tin/
(verb)

A high-level display of success demonstrated through lifestyle, possessions, or accomplishments. While often associated with things like cars, jewelry, or clothing, stuntin' can also apply to how someone lives, moves, or excels. The term carries a positive tone, reflecting confidence, recognition, and achievement.

> *The rise of "stunna shades" (oversized sunglasses worn to make a statement) reflects how stuntin' became visually tied to personal identity and presentation.*
>
> *"Bruh came through stuntin' in the old school on thangs."*

(See also: Highside)

Stupid

/stoo-pid/
(adjective)

Used to describe something excessive in a way that draws attention or admiration. Commonly applied to cars, jewelry, clothes, or anything that looks flashy, expensive, or impressive. Also used to intensify another adjective. In certain contexts, can carry an aggressive tone, often tied to sudden action or reaction.

> *"You just flipped that neck piece? That thang stupid."*
>
> *"Keep playin' wit my money you gon see me go stupid."*

(See also: Dumb, Dumb-ass, Dummy, Go Stupid, Hella)

Subin'

/sub-in/
(verb)

The exhibition of deep, heavy bass, typically from a car system or a track with strong low-end.

> "We slid through subin', wakin' the whole block up."

(See also: Bump, Knock, Pound, Slap)

Sucka

/suh-kuh/
(noun)

A coward, pushover, or individual lacking integrity, strength, or standards. Often used to describe those who are easily tricked, manipulated, or taken advantage of. In more recent usage, the term is also stylized to refer to an enemy or opposition figure.

> "We don't rock with suckas over here."
> "I seen the suckas at the light and got on em'"

Sucka Duckin'

/suh-kuh duck-in/
(verb)

Actively avoiding untrustworthy or undesirable individuals.

> "You know me, out here hustlin' and sucka duckin', mayne."

(See also: Sucka Free)

Sucka Free

/suh-kuh free/
(adjective)

Disassociating from low-character individuals; maintaining distance from those who lack integrity or respect. Also used as a colloquial or stylized name for San Francisco, due to the shared S.F. initials.

> Sometimes alternatively phrased as "busta free."
>
> "I stick wit a chosen few and stay sucka free at all times."
>
> "We out here in the Sucka Free, chillin' by the bay."

(See also: Sucka Duckin')

Sucka Repellent

/suh-kuh ruh-pel-uhnt/
(noun)

A metaphorical "spray" used to ward off undesirables, symbolizing an attitude or demeanor that naturally repels those who don't meet a certain standard. It reflects a mindset of avoiding negative influences and only engaging with individuals of a certain caliber.

> "I don't entertain nonsense. I keep that sucka repellent on me at all times."

Sucka S***

/suh-kuh s***/
(noun)

Actions that reflect weakness, disloyalty, cowardice, or a lack of integrity. Often used to call out violations of spoken or unspoken codes of conduct, especially surrounding loyalty, authenticity, or respect. The behavior of a sucka.

> "His potna was gettin' jumped and bra just gon sit up there and record. Straight sucka s***."

Sucka Standby

/suh-kuh stand-by/
(phrase)

Being left waiting for an excessively long period, often implying that one has been taken advantage of, overlooked, or treated as less important.

> "I been waitin' on you for 45 minutes. You got me on sucka standby."

Suspect

/suh-spekt/
(adjective)

Questionable in trustworthiness, integrity, or intent; often used to describe someone suspected of being weak, unreliable, or dishonest. The term can extend to calling into question a person's confidence, masculinity, or sexuality.

> "I don't know about bruh, he out here movin' real suspect."

Swang

/swang/
(verb)

To swing or drift a car in circles (donuts).

> "Yo car runnin', swang one, one time."

(See also: Donut)

Sweet One

/sweet wuhn/
(noun)

A marijuana cigarette laced with powder cocaine.

> "Bruh lit up a Sweet One and was on tilt the rest of the night."

(See also: Cavi, Grimmy)

Swoop

/swoop/
(verb)

To pick up or collect someone in a vehicle.

> "You need a ride to work? I'ma come swoop you right quick."

(See also: Scoop, Snatch)

T-Rolled

/tee-rohld/
(verb)

To be stopped, discovered, or apprehended, especially in a sudden or unexpected manner.

> "I almost got away wit it, but I got T-rolled at the last minute."

(See also: Rolled Up)

Tacked Out

/takt owt/
(adjective)

High off marijuana, often from hotboxing, smoking in a closed space like a car with the windows up, and sometimes the heater on.

> *Thought to be derived from "stuck," as in physically or mentally frozen from an intense high, with "tack" suggesting something pinned down or stuck in place.*
>
> "Bruh was tacked out in the backseat, eyes barely open."

Take Flight

/tayk flyt/
(verb phrase)

To strike first in a fight, usually with no warning. Refers to the moment someone initiates physical conflict, often as a response to disrespect or rising tension.

> "He kept talkin', so bruh had to take flight on him."

(See also: Fired On, Get Off Where You Mad At, Stole On, Take Off)

Take Off

/tayk awf/
(verb phrase)

To attack or punch.

> "If bra even look at me wrong I'ma take off."

(See also: Fired On, Get Off Where You Mad At, Stole On, Take Flight)

Talk Baseball

/tawk bayse-bawl/
(phrase)

A cue to switch the subject, often preceded by "kill game." Used to discreetly steer the conversation to something harmless or unrelated.

> "Here she come, kill game, talk baseball."

(See also: Kill Game)

Tap In

/tap in/
(verb phrase)

To reach out, make contact, or check in with someone.

> "I got a play up, tap in wit me."

(See also: Hit Me On The Hip, Hit My Line, Holla)

Task

/tassk/
(noun)

The Oakland Task Force, a tactical police unit popularized in the crack-era for their zero-tolerance, and often abusive enforcement tactics.

> *Often pronounced "Tass."*
> *"If you run from task and get caught, you fasho gettin' whooped."*

(See also: 5-O, The Boys, Po Po, The Rollers)

Taxin'

/tak-sin/
(verb)

Charging a high or exorbitant price, often seen as unfair or excessive.

> *"Bruh taxin' for them shoes."*

Tellin'

/tel-in/
(verb)

A colloquial term for snitching; giving up information to authorities, usually under pressure or after being caught.

> *"Soon as they snatched him up he start tellin'."*

Tenda

/ten-duh/
(noun)

A Bay Area pronunciation of "tender," used to describe an extremely attractive or desirable person.

> Possibly short for or derived from "tenderoni."
>
> "I'm bout to pull up on this lil tenda out in Berkeley right quick."

(See also: Chassy, Top Notch)

Test Your Pimpin'

/tes ya pimp-in/
(verb phrase)

To call into question, or challenge someone's ability or authenticity, in an attempt to force them to prove themselves.

> "Don't test my pimpin' bra, you know how I'm movin'."

Thang

/thayng/
(noun)

A flexible term that can refer to a firearm, a kilo of cocaine, or serve as a general catch-all depending on context.

> "Lil dude can't come in 'less he leave the thang in the car."
>
> "Bra got jacked by 5-0, he had two pistols and a thang in the trunk."

(See also: Big Thang, Cannon, Hammer, Kick, Thumper)

Thangs

/thayngz/
(noun)

An abbreviation of "Gold Thangs," referring to gold-plated wire-spoke wheels.

> "They gon really jock when I pull up on thangs."

(See also: Gold Ones, Gold Thangs)

That Go

/that goh/
(phrase)

An affirming way to say something is good, appealing, or well done. Often used in response to food, music, outfits, or anything that stands out in a positive way. Related to Go, but used as a statement of approval rather than a descriptive verb.

> "You just made that beat last night? That go."

(See also: Go)

That Thang
/that thayng/
(noun)

A versatile placeholder term for anything the speaker wants to highlight or call attention to. The phrase can appear as either that thang or this thang, with the choice depending on sentence structure or perspective. Highly context-dependent, it does not refer to a specific object or activity; instead, it serves as a colloquial way of saying "that thing", whatever the speaker finds relevant or significant in the moment.

> "I heard that new E-40, he lightweight gassin' on that thang."

(See also: G-Thang, Thang)

Thick
/thik/
(adjective)

Refers to a body type characterized by a curvaceous and full-figured lower body, particularly emphasizing voluptuousness below the waist. This term is usually used in reference to women.

> "Her face ain't that cool, but she fakeway thick though."

Thizz
/thiz/
(noun)

A slang term for the drug ecstasy (MDMA).

> "Bruh was off a thizz at the function last night."

Thizz Face

/thiz fayss/
(noun phrase)

The exaggerated facial expression made after taking ecstasy (MDMA), usually characterized by scrunched features, squinting eyes, and clenched jaw.

> "Bruh popped a pill and hit the thizz face on stage."

(See also: Thizz)

Thizzin'

/thiz-in/
(verb)

To be high on ecstasy (MDMA) or to display its effects, which can include noticeable physical or behavioral signs.

> "Bruh was at the function dumb-ass thizzin' last night."

(See also: Thizz, Thizz Face)

Thizzle

/thiz-uhl/
(noun)

A playful or stylized substitute for the word thang, often used to encourage someone to handle their business or express confidence in what they're doing.

> "Bruh out here doin' his thizzle."

Tho

/doe/
(adverb)

A colloquial contraction of "though," commonly placed at the end of a sentence to add emphasis, reinforce a statement, or subtly contrast an idea in a casual, conversational tone.

> Often pronounced "doe" in Oakland vernacular.
>
> "I'm ready to cut tho."
>
> "This food smackin' tho."
>
> "Man, I'm just sayin' tho."

Thou-Wow

/thow-wow/
(noun)

A term for one thousand, often used in reference to money, or to emphasize a high level of authenticity, or realness.

> "I ain't even gon lie, she a real one. Straight up, she always keep it a thou-wow."

(See also: Band, Bandaid, Keep It Funky, One Hunnid, Rack)

Thru

/throo/
(adjective)

Worn out, neglected, or less than presentable, suggesting a decline in appearance or condition.

> "You need some new kicks, them ones you got is thru."

Thru Wit Money

/throo wit muh-nee/
(adjective)

An extension of thru, used to describe someone or something as completely finished, done for, or beyond repair. It can also express shock or disbelief so strong it makes someone disregard all else of value.

> *"Girl, who you let in yo head? You look thru wit money."*

Thug It Out

/thuhg it owt/
(phrase)

To endure or persevere through difficult or challenging situations with resilience and toughness, often suggesting a tough, no-excuses approach to facing adversity.

> *"I knew it was the wrong decision, now I just gotta thug it out."*

Thumper

/thuhm-per/
(noun)

A gun or firearm.

> *"He runnin' around wit that thumper on him."*

(See also: Cannon, Hammer, Thang)

Tight

/tite/
(adjective)

Used to describe something as cool, impressive, or of high quality.

> "You see that Chevelle? That thang tight."

Tight Ones

/tyt wunz/
(noun)

Compact and precise donuts performed during car maneuvers, often seen in sideshows where drivers perform tight circular drifts.

> "He turnt a couple tight ones and got up outta there."

(See also: Donut, Swang)

To The Face

/tuh thuh fayss/
(phrase)

Alone or by yourself.

> "She had a whole pizza to the face."

(See also: Bolo, To The Neck)

To The Neck
/tuh thuh nek/
(phrase)

By oneself or alone.

> *"Everybody gone for the day, I got the house to the neck."*

(See also: Bolo, To The Face)

Top Hat
/top-hat/
(noun)

An individual regarded as being in a position of high status or esteem. The term marks someone as belonging to the upper echelon, whether through wealth, influence, or the respect they command, and is often used to acknowledge those seen as prominent or elite.

> *"Bruh walk in the room like a real top hat, everybody showin' respect."*

(See also: Boss)

Top Notch
/top nach/
(noun)

A person, typically a woman, considered extremely beautiful or attractive. Often used to describe a "9" or "10" in casual rankings of beauty, implying not just physical appeal but also status and desirability.

> Sometimes phrased as "notch."

> *"Bruh slid through wit a Top Notch; had everybody turnin' they head."*

(See also: Chassy, Tenda)

Toss Up

/taws uhp/
(noun)

A promiscuous or sexually indiscriminate woman.

> "You don't wanna make her your main, she a old school toss up."

(See also: Bopper, Ripper, Runner)

The Town

/thuh town/
(noun)

A widely used nickname for Oakland, California.

> Derived from the earlier term "Oaktown," The Town has become the most popular and enduring way locals refer to the city.

> "Bruh been reppin' The Town heavy since the '90s."

(See also: Oaktown, The "O")

Town Business

/town biz-nis/
(phrase)

A term used to describe activities or behaviors typical of, representing, or associated with Oakland, California, often referred to as "The Town."

> "Cuzzo just flipped a Skylark. I tried to tell him that ain't Town business."

(See also: City Situation)

Toys
/toyz/
(noun)

Recreational possessions, often expensive or high-end. Most commonly refers to vehicles like bikes, cars, or boats, but can also extend to other items. Typically implies having more than one.

> "Bra out here ballin', he got toys."

Traffic
/traf-ik/
(phrase)

Public spaces where people are out and about, often casually or socially, with the possibility of running into others.

> "I don't have her new number, but I'm sure I'll see her in traffic."

Treat Your Nose
/treet yohr nohz/
(verb phrase)

To snort cocaine.

> *A euphemism commonly used to downplay or indirectly reference drug use.*
>
> "He be in the back treatin' his nose damn near every time we pull up."

(See also: Playin' Wit Your Nose)

Tremendo

/tre-men-doh/
(noun, adjective)

Refers to a car stereo system with deep bass and heavy sound output, typically built around large subwoofers. Commonly used for setups that meet or exceed the standard associated with 12- and 15-inch subs. Also used to describe the sound produced by such systems.

> *Stylized version of "tremendous."*
>
> *"Bruh pulled up with tremendo, shakin' the whole block."*

(See also: Bump, Knock, Slap, Slump)

Trippin'

/trip-in/
(verb)

To overreact, become excessively upset, or show unnecessary concern, often in situations where such behavior is unreasonable or uncalled for.

> *"Lil baby blew up on me, but I ain't even trippin'."*

Trophy

/tro-fee/
(noun)

A fixed-up classic car, often referred to as an old school, symbolizing hard work, consistency, and status. Called a trophy because it represents dedication over time and is closely tied to one's reputation. It serves as a visual testament to pride, earned respect, and consistency.

> *"Bruh been puttin' that Trophy together since high school."*

Tryna

/try-nuh/
(contraction)

Shortened form of "trying to." Common in casual speech to express intent, effort, or desire to do something.

> "I'm tryna stack this paper and stay tucked, you feel me?"

Tuck

/tuhk/
(verb)

To conceal something by placing it out of sight, often in a small or discreet location. Can also refer to withholding a portion of money owed, especially in situations where the full amount is intentionally kept back.

> "She lied about her check so she could tuck a few dollars."

Tuck Spot

/tuhk spaht/
(noun)

A hidden or secretive place used for storing and/or concealing items.

> "You need to find a lil tuck spot for your valuables."

Tucked

/tukt/
(adjective)

Concealed, low-profile, or intentionally kept out of sight. Used in reference to physical things, such as money, weapons, vehicles, stash spots, or someone laying low.

> "He keep the hammer tucked right under the seat."

(See also: Stayin' Out The Way, Tuck, Tuck Spot, Under)

Tuff

/tuhf/
(adverb)

Frequently, intensely, or with strong dedication.

> "You've been with her every day for the last two weeks. Y'all been kickin' it real tuff."

Turf

/terf/
(noun)

A specific area known for street activity, often involving drug sales, territorial presence, or reputation; generally recognized as belonging to or controlled by a certain individual or group, and understood to be their spot.

> In the Bay Area, gangs are largely absent. Instead, people identify with turfs, a term that refers both to the area and to the group of individuals from or representing that area. Though newer generations may reflect some gang-like behavior, turf culture remains distinct in structure and identity.
>
> "He been posted on the turf since high school."

Turf Dance

/terf dans/
(noun)

A form of hip-hop street dance that originated in Oakland, California. Characterized by smooth, controlled movements like gliding, waving, and contorting, it draws influence from older styles such as pop locking and boogaloo.

> "They was turf dancin' all night at the function."

(See also: Giggin', Hittin' It)

Turf Tax
/terf taks/
(noun)

A cost, consequence, or price paid as a result of operating within a particular turf or area, often in the context of hustling or street-level activity. The term can also refer to an unspoken "rent" for conducting business or occupying space on a drug turf; typically applied to those without proper standing, though not exclusively.

> "He thought he could post up without checking in, now he paying that turf tax."

Turnt Up
/turnt uhp/
(adjective)

Extremely energized, excited, or stimulated, often in the context of parties, events, or confrontations. It can also refer to being increased, upgraded, or elevated in some capacity, typically due to a rise in income or status, often through the influence or support of someone else.

> Often abbreviated as "turnt."
>
> While not native to the Bay Area, Turnt Up is one of the few widely adopted non-regional terms that gained traction locally due to its compatibility with Bay energy and culture.
>
> "The function was turnt up last night."
>
> "The argument got heated, and he was turnt all the way up."

(See also: Hyphy)

Tweakin'

/twee-kin/
(verb)

Speaking or acting in an undesirable way, often under the influence of drugs.

> *"You on one, bra. Exactly what is you tweakin' off?"*

(See also: Geekin')

Twist

/twist/
(noun)

A deceptive plan, scheme, or situation intended to mislead, manipulate, or get over on someone. Can refer to either the act of deception or the environment surrounding it.

> *"You always tryin' to twist."*
>
> *"He got caught up in a twist."*

(See also: Dangler, Fadangle)

Twisted

/twis-tid/
(adjective)

Describes a state of being misunderstood, misjudged, or disrespected, often in a way that calls for correction.

> Commonly used in the phrase "you got me twisted" to challenge false assumptions or check someone's tone.
>
> "You got me twisted, potna."
>
> "She not my type, but don't get it twisted, I'd still date her."

(See also: Bent)

Twomp

/twomp/
(noun)

Twenty (often referencing $20).

> "I gave him a twomp on the gas tho."

(See also: Dub)

Twomp Sack

/twomp sak/
(noun)

A $20 bag of marijuana.

> The word "twomp" is derived from the number twenty and, while often used in reference to the dollar amount, it can also represent the number 20 more broadly.
>
> "I'm just tryna grab a lil twomp sack for the night."

(See also: Bomb, Dank, Dub, Gas, Purple)

U-ey
/yoo-ee/
(noun)

A U-turn; refers to the driving maneuver of turning around to head in the opposite direction.

> "He missed the exit and had to bust a uey."

Ugly
/ug-lee/
(adjective)

A quick way to say something is bad, negative, or not going right. Similar to saying it's not looking good. Can also be used as a flat "no."

> "You comin' out tonight?" "Nah, it's ugly."

> "It's ugly, they just hit bruh with the kickstand."

(See also: It's All Bad)

Ugly Cuz
/ug-lee kuzz/
(noun)

A joking or playful way of saying "cousin" or "cuzzin," often used between friends or acquaintances. Typically said in jest, with no actual offense intended.

> "Chill out, ugly cuz; you trippin' right now."

Uhhh

/uhhh/
(exclamation)

A drawn-out sound effect used to represent a quick escape, sudden shift, or reversal. Often mimicking the motion of turning a corner, dodging something, or backing out abruptly.

> *"I saw them boys posted on the corner so I hit the uey like, uhhh, and slid off."*
>
> *"They was about to get on the kid, I had to, uhhh, get little on em, you feel me."*

Under Spot

/un-duh spaht/
(noun phrase)

A location someone prefers not to reveal, usually to keep it low-key or exclusive. May refer to a restaurant, shop, or any place considered too good to share. Often used to protect a favorite spot from becoming too popular or crowded.

> *Often phrased as "Lil Unda Spot."*
>
> *"Where you get them saucy kicks at, bruh?" "Lil unda spot..."*

(See also: Ducked Off, Under)

Under

/uhn-duh/
(adjective)

Actions or behaviors that are low-key, inconspicuous, or conducted quietly, often with a deliberate effort to avoid attention.

> *Sometimes shortened to "un."*
> *Commonly pronounced "unda," derived from "undercover."*
> *"Bruh always keepin' it under, he stay up out the mix."*

Under Bucket

/uhn-duh buck-it/
(noun)

An inconspicuous, inexpensive, often worn-down car used to avoid drawing attention. Typically chosen for blending in or staying low-key.

> *"He drives an unda bucket to keep a low profile."*

Under Mobby

/uhn-duh mah-bee/
(noun)

An inconspicuous, functional car, typically used to avoid drawing attention. Often more intact or respectable than an under bucket, but still chosen for low-key movement without attracting notice.

> *"She slid through in the under mobby; kept it all the way discreet."*

V-Town
/vee town/
(noun)

An alternate name for Vallejo, California, used in speech, music, and local slang. Sometimes simply called The V.

"She said she from V-Town, born and raised."

(See also: Valley Jo)

Valley Jo
/val-ee joh/
(noun)

A commonly used nickname for Vallejo, California, often heard in conversation and regional references.

"A lot of real ones came outta that Valley Jo."

(See also: V-Town)

Vicious
/vi-shus/
(adjective)

Powerfully impressive, striking, or dominating in appearance or presence, often with an aggressive edge that commands attention.

"That jewelry setup is vicious."

W.S.O.

/dub-uhl-yoo ess oh/
(initialism, noun)

Initialism for West Side Oakland. Rarely spoken but sometimes seen in graffiti or written references to West Oakland.

> "Somebody sprayed W.S.O. on the bathroom wall."

(See also: E.S.O., N.S.O.)

Wake Em Up

/wayk um up/
(verb phrase)

Forcing people to recognize your value, skills, or presence, often in response to being overlooked or underestimated. Can also refer to playing music at an extremely high volume, often with heavy bass, to make sure it is noticed.

> "They was sleepin' on me, so I had to wake em up."
>
> "I slid through the block wit 4 15's, wakin' em up."

(See also: Bump, Knock, Slap, Wake Ya Game Up)

Wake Ya Game Up
/wayk yuh gaym up/
(phrase)

To come to a realization or gain a deeper understanding, whether through personal insight, being informed, or another influencing factor.

> Also phrased as "Wake Up Ya Game."
>
> "He was movin' reckless, so I had to wake his game up before he got caught up."

(See also: Wake Em Up)

Washed
/wawsht/
(adjective)

Being sentenced to a very long term in prison, often life.

> "They washed bra at court yesterday; hit him wit the kickstand."

(See also: Elroy, Kickstand, "L")

Way-Way
/way-way/
(noun)

The freeway.

> "I'm finna jump on the way-way, I'll be there in 15 minutes."

Weak

/week/
(adjective)

Overcome with laughter, typically in response to something extremely funny.

> "Bruh scrubbed tryin' to hit that wheely; had me weak."

Weak Move

/week moov/
(noun phrase)

An action or decision that reflects poor judgment, lack of integrity, or a failure to uphold respected social codes. Often considered premature, unwise, unethical, or non-player behavior, especially in situations where dignity, loyalty, or game are expected.

> "He went out and made a weak move 'cause he was in his feelings."

(See also: Sucka S***)

Weenie

/wee-nee/
(noun)

A coward or pushover; someone easily intimidated, manipulated, or lacking in courage or assertiveness. Often used to dismiss or belittle individuals who fail to stand up for themselves or who avoid confrontation.

> "Bruh folded the second they pressed him; straight weenie."

(See also: Busta, Mark, Poodle)

Weird

/weerd/
(adjective)

Different or "extra" in an unflattering or undesirable way. Often used to describe someone moving in a distasteful, awkward, or inappropriate manner. Can function as a catch-all term for actions or behavior seen as undesirable, questionable, or socially off-putting.

> "You left me hangin' the other night, you weird, bro."

Went Down

/went down/
(verb phrase)

Having been arrested or taken to jail. Often used when someone is caught in connection to a crime.

> Alternatively phrased as "took down."
>
> "Bruh went down for a hot one."
>
> "He got took down in broad daylight."

The West

/thuh west/
(noun)

An informal name for West Oakland, California. Refers to the section of Oakland located west of downtown, roughly bounded by Interstate 580 to the north, Interstate 980 to the east, and the Port of Oakland and San Francisco Bay to the west. Known for its rich history in Black culture, political activism, and music, The West has long been a hub for both community pride and street reputation. The term is often used to express local identity or to reference the area in cultural, social, and street-related contexts.

> *"It was a function up at Defermery; seemed like the whole west was out there."*

(See also: W.S.O.)

Wet

/wet/
(adjective)

Something or someone that is exceptionally nice looking, polished, or impressive. A term likely influenced by the sleek, glossy finish of well-done car paint.

> *"I ain't never seen them J's before, them thangs wet."*

(See also: Clean, Saucy)

What You Got Up?

/wut yoo got up/
(phrase)

A casual way of asking about someone's plans or what they have going on, often used to check in or start a conversation about the day's activities.

> "What you got up for today, Family?"

What You On?

/wut yoo awn/
(phrase)

Slang for asking what someone is doing, planning, or involved in. Can refer to immediate actions or general life updates. Also commonly used to question someone's behavior, especially if they are being overly sensitive, acting strangely, or moving aggressively or inappropriately.

> "What you on later? Tryna link?"
> "What you on, bruh? You trippin'."

What-It-Do

/wut it doo/
(phrase)

Originally a request for drivers to showcase the capabilities of their cars (e.g., "Show me what it do!"). Over time, "What-It-Do" has evolved into a versatile slang term, similar to "What's up?" It is often used rhetorically to express agreement or readiness to engage in a proposed action, serving as a casual greeting or an enthusiastic response to a challenge or suggestion.

> A popular reply, "What it don't do," suggests that the person is open and ready for anything, emphasizing a readiness to engage in any and all activities.
>
> "What it do, Family?"

(See also: What's Hatnin' Wit It, What's Up Wit Blud, What's Up Wit It)

Whatever

/wuh-dev-er/
(phrase)

A catch-all placeholder used to simplify or sidestep complex thoughts, concepts, or actions, often when something doesn't need to be spelled out. Distinct from other Bay Area placeholders like woo wop or you feel me, it frequently carries undertones of deception, manipulation, or doing something on the sly. In essence, it's a way of pointing to what's going on without breaking down the psychology behind it.

> "He came through on the whatever tip, thinkin' I wouldn't notice."
>
> "You tryin' to whatever me?"
>
> "Lil baby tried to pull a whatever; thought she was gon' whatever me tho."

(See also: G-Thang, Woo Wop, You Feel Me)

Whatizit

/wuh-diz-it/
(phrase)

A stylized form of "what is it," used as a greeting. Often rhetorical, but can also function as a vague check-in depending on tone, similar to asking what's going on or what the plan is.

> "Whatizit, a blizzard?"

(See also: What-It-Do, What's Hatnin' Wit It, What's Really, What's Up Wit Blud)

What's Hatnin'

/wuts hat-nin/
(phrase)

A regional variation of "What's happening?" used as a greeting or to ask what's going on.

> *Characterized by its distinct Bay Area pronunciation of "happening" as "hatnin'," this phrase carries local flavor and familiarity.*
>
> "Ayy, what's hatnin', loved one?"

(See also: What's Hatnin' Wit It, What's Up Wit Blud, What's Up Wit It, What-It-Do)

What's Hatnin' Wit It

/wuts hat-nin wit it/
(phrase)

An extended variation of "What's Hatnin'," used to greet someone or ask what's going on. The phrase carries a familiar, conversational tone and is distinctly rooted in Bay Area slang.

> "Ayy, what's hatnin' wit it, brody? You good?"

(See also: What-It-Do, What's Really, What's Up Wit Blud, What's Up Wit It)

What's Really

/wuts reel-ee/
(phrase)

A casual greeting or inquiry used to ask what's going on or how someone is doing. Commonly understood as a shortened form of What's Really Good? Often used semi-rhetorically, not necessarily expecting a detailed answer.

> "Hey, what's up y'all, what's really?"

(See also: What's Hatnin' Wit It, What's Up Wit Blud, What's Up Wit It)

What's Up Wit Blud

/wuhssup wit bluhd/
(phrase)

A casual way to ask someone, "What's up with you?" Often used to check in on a person's well-being or activities.

> "I ain't seen you in a minute, what's up wit blud?"

(See also: What's Hatnin' Wit It, What's Really, What's Up Wit It, What-It-Do)

What's Up Wit It
/wuhssup wit it/
(phrase)

A casual greeting or inquiry about a situation, similar to "what's up?" but with an added sense of engagement.

> "What's up wit it, loved one?"

(See also: What's Hatnin' Wit It, What's Really, What's Up Wit Blud, What-It-Do)

Whip
/whip/
(verb)

To fix up, customize, or restore something, often to a high standard of appearance or style.

> In broader slang, the term also refers to a car or automobile.
>
> "I'm finna whip the 'Stang soon as my settlement come through."

Whipped
/whipt/
(adjective)

Describes something that has been done up, styled, or refined to a high standard of appearance. Implies polish, care, and attention to detail, suggesting it has been properly "whipped" or finished to perfection.

> "Your hair look whipped, who hooked you?"

(See also: Clean, Saucy, Whip)

Whistle Tip
/whis-uhl tip/
(noun)

A modified vehicle exhaust pipe that produces a high-pitched whistling sound during operation. Common in scraper car culture and closely tied to the Hyphy movement, where the sound became a signature element of the scene's style and attitude.

> *"I'm hella glad whistle tips played out."*

(See also: The Hyphy Movement, Scraper)

Whoride
/hoo-ride/
(noun, verb)

To act disruptively or aggressively in a public setting, often causing a scene or confrontation. Can also refer to teasing or mocking someone in a way that stirs things up. As a noun, describes a chaotic or disruptive event marked by aggressive behavior or a public disturbance.

> *Alternatively spelled "Hooride."*
>
> *"He came up there whoridin', yellin' and kickin' tables."*
>
> *"She whorided him about his mobby, and everybody joined in."*
>
> *"Everyone was yelling and throwing punches; the whole night ended in a whoride."*

Wiggle

/wig-uhl/
(verb)

To leave or move from one place to another. Can also refer to staying active, moving around in pursuit of opportunity, or hustling.

> "You ain't gon' come up sittin' still; you gotta get out here and wiggle."

(See also: Bounce, Do It Movin', Get Little, Shake The Spot, Windy)

Windy

/win-dee/
(adjective)

Leaving or departing from a place. Often used to describe someone who has left quickly or is no longer present.

> "Soon as the law pulled up we got windy."

(See also: Bounce, Do It Movin', Get Little, Shake The Spot, Wiggle)

Wit The Movement

/wit thuh moov-ment/
(phrase)

A way of describing someone who is being overly hyphy or acting undesirably, often by drawing unnecessary attention, behaving erratically, or going over the top in a social setting. The phrase references the Hyphy Movement and is typically said directly to the offending party to call out their behavior.

> "Bruh, you need to chill out, you wit the movement right now."

(See also: Doin' Too Much, Extra, Trippin')

Wit The S***

/wit thuh s***/
(phrase)

Describes someone willing to engage in criminal, violent, or reckless behavior, or someone acting irrationally, confrontationally, or mischievously.

> *In some regions, this phrase is often heard as "Wit The S***s." This appears to be a mishearing of the original West Coast usage rather than an intentional regional reinterpretation.*
>
> *"Don't test bruh pimpin', he one-thousand percent wit the s***."*

(See also: Active, Extra, Trippin', Wit The Movement)

Wolf Tickets

/woolf tik-its/
(noun)

Lies told boastfully to deceive or intimidate; a false promise.

> *Some trace the phrase to a scene in the 1974 film The Education of Sonny Carson, where a gang leader named Wolf is told to "quit selling the tickets." This could suggest a possible origin or popularization of the term.*
>
> *"Bruh stay sellin' wolf tickets; he ain't about none of that."*

(See also: Wolfin')

Wolfin'

/wool-fin/
(verb)

Talking big with no intention to follow through. Often refers to exaggerating, bluffing, or making empty threats to impress or intimidate.

> "Ain't nobody trippin' off blud. He just wolfin' again."

(See also: Wolf Tickets)

Woo Wop

/woo-wahp/
(noun)

A catch-all placeholder used to refer to any thing, situation, item, or activity, whether specific or general. Often used when the speaker doesn't want to be exact or when the meaning is understood from context.

> *Sometimes phrased as "woopty wop."*
> "We brought the food, drinks, and music, the whole lil woo wop."
> "5-0 got behind me. Luckily, I had tucked the lil woo wop under the seat."

Work

/wurk/
(noun)

A current or potential love interest, often emphasizing attractiveness; can also refer to drugs for sale.

> "The club was movin' last night; it was work in that thang."
> "He just re-upped, so he got work right now."

Ya Hemi

/ya heh-mee/
(phrase)

A colloquial way of saying "You hear me?" or "Do you understand?" Often used for emphasis, confirmation, to check if someone is following what's being said, or simply as a rhetorical filler.

> "I told him it's real business only, ya hemi?"

(See also: Ya Understand Me, You Feel Me)

Ya Understand Me

/yuh unda-stan mee/
(phrase)

A common phrase in Oakland, Bay-Area slang, similar in nature to "ya know what I'm sayin'." This expression, a phonetic alteration of "you understand me," is often used at the end of statements. While it can serve to ensure the listener grasps the speaker's point or perspective, it is frequently employed as a rhetorical filler, habitually used to engage the listener or emphasize the conversation's flow.

> *Like much of Oakland's slang, its origins trace back to pimp culture.*
> "I'm out here movin' mean, ya understand me?"

(See also: Ya Hemi, You Feel Me)

Yadadamean

/ya-da-da-meen/
(expression)

A stylized one-word version of "you know what I mean," used for emphasis, confirmation, or punctuation in speech.

> Sometimes shortened to "yadada."
>
> "We slid through deep, had the whole spot jumpin', yadadamean?"

(See also: Ya Hemi, Ya Understand Me, You Feel Me)

Yank

/yank/
(verb)

To pull out a firearm, usually a pistol; also used to describe pulling up or arriving in a vehicle, or to describe a scene becoming active, lively, or exciting.

> "Bruh was talkin' slick, so he yanked on him."
>
> "We just yanked up to the function."
>
> "The party about to yank."

(See also: Yankin')

Yank Up

/yank uhp/
(verb phrase)

To pull up or arrive somewhere in a vehicle, often suddenly or with noticeable presence.

> "We just yanked up to the function around midnight."

(See also: Slide, Yank, Yankin')

Yankee

/yang-kee/
(adjective, verb)

A Bay Area expression related to yankin', used to describe something good, impressive, or extreme.

> *Sometimes phrased as "yankees," not necessarily as a plural but as an alternate form with the same sense.*
>
> "I'm finna go yankee out here, watch how I put this together."
>
> "The function went yankee last night."
>
> "The paint on the old school wet, that thang goin' yankees."

(See also: Go Dumb, Go Stupid, Yank, Yankin')

Yankin'

/yank-in/
(adjective, verb)

Describes an event or situation that's energetic, crowded, or going well. Often used to describe a party, function, or street scene that's active and drawing attention.

> "This party yankin' right now."

(See also: Yank)

Yaper

/yay-per/
(noun)

A slang term created through a phonetic alteration where the initial consonant of words like "paper" or "taper" is replaced with 'y.' This form of word modification usually refers to money when derived from "paper," or a type of haircut when derived from "taper," etc.

> "On errythang, that boy havin' yaper."
>
> "I'm bout to slide up to the shop and get yapered up."

Yay Area

/yay air-ee-uh/
(noun)

A phonetic alteration of Bay Area, rooted in the slang term yayo (cocaine). The name reflects the region's deep connection to both street culture and the drug trade during the crack era. Often used with pride or playfulness to represent the Bay in music and conversation.

> "You already know where I'm from, the Yay Area."

Yay Yay
/yay-yay/
(verb phrase)

A Bay Area expression meaning crazy or going crazy. The phrase can carry different tones depending on context, from positive and hype to confrontational or even negative.

> "The afterparty went yay yay."
>
> "She pulled up hella hyphy, hopped out the car goin' yay yay."
>
> "That beat goin' yay yay."

(See also: Go Dumb, Go Stupid, Yankin')

Yeee!
/yeee/
(exclamation)

A spirited shout or cheer used throughout the Bay Area to express excitement or agreement, but notably absent in Oakland culture.

> Believed to have originated in Richmond, California, specifically within the Kennedy Manor housing projects.
>
> "We was dumb-ass turnt up at the lil function last night, like yeee!"

(See also: Ayyy)

Yikin'

/yike-in/
(verb)

Can refer to a slightly more reserved form of yokin', where the driver quickly alternates the accelerator and brake to rock the car back and forth, or to a dance that simulates intercourse.

> "Lil bruh pullt up in the Chev, yikin' that thang."

(See also: Yokin')

Yiny

/yai-nee/
(adjective)

A phonetic alteration of "tiny."

> "That shirt kinda yiny bra."

(See also: Young)

Yistol

/yiss-tol/
(noun)

Phonetic alteration of "pistol."

> "It's gettin' kinda spunky out here. I been keepin' this lil yistol wit me at all times."

(See also: Hammer, Thang, Thumper)

Yittadit

/yit-uh-dit/
(noun)

Slang reference to a woman.

> "I'm bout to go snatch up this lil yittadit right quick."

The Yoc

/thuh yahk/
(noun)

Antioch, California. An infrequently used regional nickname, occasionally heard within the Bay Area.

> "Cuzzo got people out in The Yoc."

Yokin'

/yoh-kin/
(verb)

Quickly alternating the accelerator and brake, causing the car to rock back and forth, often lifting the front wheel off the ground.

> "Bruh came through yokin' the Delt so hard that thang was liftin' off the ground."

(See also: Yikin')

You Feel Me

/yoo feel mee/
(phrase)

A rhetorical question used to ask for agreement or understanding, similar to "ya understand me" or "ya know what I'm sayin'." Also used as a placeholder for unspecified or indirectly mentioned things, avoiding saying something directly.

> "I got the lobster wit the crab, the butter, the whole lil you feel me."
>
> "I was hella tired at work today, but I gotta keep grinding, you feel me?"
>
> "My BM text, but I ain't hit back cause I was ridin' with the new lil you feel me."

(See also: Ya Hemi, Ya Understand Me)

You Got Me F****d Up

/yoo got mee f****d up/
(phrase)

An expression of indignation or refusal; implies someone's perception of you is incorrect or disrespectful.

> "You think I'm gon do all the work while you take all the credit? You got me f****d up."

You See It
/yoo see it/
(expression)

A playful, self-assured response when someone notices or comments on a possession, usually something stylish, flashy, or valuable. Typically said with light sarcasm or humor, to casually acknowledge the attention without sounding like you're bragging.

> "That watch bussin', bruh." "You see it."

Young
/yuhng/
(adjective)

Used to describe something that is small or undersized. Most often refers to clothing that fits tight or looks too small, but can also be used to describe portions, amounts, or payments that feel lacking or light.

> "That shirt saucy, but it's kinda young, bra."

(See also: Yiny)

Young Life
/yung lyfe/
(noun)

A term used by an older man to refer to a younger male under his guidance, influence, or informal mentorship. Typically denotes a younger friend or protégé who can be relied on for tasks, favors, or to take action when called upon.

> "My young life quick to rock up on somethin, straight hyphy."

(See also: Youngsta)

Youngsta

/yung-stuh/
(noun)

A casual term for someone considered part of a younger generation. Often refers to a teen or someone in their early adulthood, but can be applied more broadly to highlight a noticeable age gap or difference in experience.

> "These youngstas don't know nothin' about that old school game, mayne."

(See also: Young Life)

Zap

/zap/
(noun)

An in-car equalizer made by Zapco, highly prized in 1980s-1990s Bay Area car culture for enhancing sound systems. Associated with old school rides featuring heavy bass, custom paint jobs, and gold-spoked rims. Owners often kept the unit loose on their lap while driving, giving rise to sayings like "Zap on my lap."

> "O.G. pulled up saucy, candy paint, on thangs, wit the zap on his lap."

Zark

/zark/
(noun)

Phonetic alteration of mark.

> "I ain't foolin' wit bra, he a straight up zark."

(See also: Mark)

Zip

/zip/
(noun)

An ounce of drugs, typically used to measure substances like marijuana or cocaine.

> "I need a half a zip right quick."

(See also: Zone)

Zone

/zohn/
(noun)

Another term for an ounce of drugs, commonly used in transactions and discussions involving substances like marijuana.

> *"I'm 'bout to pull up and snatch a zone right quick."*

(See also: Zip)

Z's & V's

/zeez n veez/
(noun)

Short for "Zeniths and Vogues," a popular pairing of aftermarket car rims (Zenith wire wheels) and luxury whitewall tires (Vogue Tyres), often associated with custom cars and street culture.

> *"Bruh pulled up clean on them Z's & V's."*

THEMATIC INDEX

Substances & Drugs (67)
A1 Yola, B'La, Bammer, Belushi, Bo, Bomb, Bundle, Cavi, Chop, Cola, Cream, Cryp, D, Dank, Doja, Dope Fiend, Dope Fiends, Double Up, Drank, Gas, Geekin', Good, Grandaddy, Grapes, Grimmy, Gurpin', Half Thang, Heem, Hop, Hotbox, Hubba, Indo, Kick, L.G., Lit, Loaded, Nade, Noid, Nose Job, Out My Body, PC, Pae Pae, Pervin', Pickle, Playin' Wit Your Nose, Pow Wow, Powda, Powderhead, Purple, Rollin', Sack, Servin', Slumped, Smacked, Smoke, Stuck, Sweet One, Thizz, Thizzin', Thizzle, To The Face, Treat Your Nose, Tweakin', Twomp Sack, Work, Zip, Zone

Behavior & Actions (60)
Bolo, Buff, Cat Off, Check, Come-A-New, Cool On, Do The Damn Thang, Do The Fool, Doin' The Most, Doin' Too Much, Ducked Off, Extra, Extra'd Out, Fake, Fake Feelin' It, Fake Kick It, Fake Nutty, Funny Style, Geesin', Get Back, Get Down, Get It, Get On, Go Out, Hatin', Hush Mode, In Pocket, In The Way, Left Hangin', Mainy, Marinate, Mean Mug, Move Mean, Nut Up, Nutty, On Some Other S***, On The Hush, On Your Bumper, Outside, Outta Pocket, Push A (Hard) Line, Put In Check, Salibone, Sav It Out, Scrub, Smash Artist, Stayin' Out The Way, Steppin' On S***, Stick To The Script, Sucka Duckin', Sucka S***, Thug It Out, Trippin', Tucked, Tweakin', Under, Weird, Whoride, Wit The Movement, Wit The S***

Money & Finance (60)
A Lil Bit of Nothin', Ballin', Ballin' Out Of Control, Band, Bandaid, Bank, Banked Up, Break, Break Bread, Bubble, Caked Up, Cash Me Out, Cash Out, Cent, Check, Come Up, D-Boy Knot, Doin' Bad, Dolla, Dub, Dusted & Disgusted, Fetti, Financially Embarrassed, Five Finger Discount, Flip, For The F, Get Back, Get Your Money On, Gettin It, Grip, Havin' It, Hit A Lick, Hooked, Hunnid, Issue, Joog, Kick Me Down, Lash, Mail, Mil-Ticket, Off, Paper, Papered Up, Plug, Pockets Touchin', Posted, Quarter Spoon, Rack, Run Mine, Skrilla, Soft, Stack, Struck, Stung, Taxin', Thou-Wow, Thru Wit Money, Tuck, Twomp, Yaper

THEMATIC INDEX

Violence, Fighting & Conflict (56)
Aired Out, Bank, Banked On, Boop Bop, Burners, Chunk 'Em, Demo, Dipped, Downt, Fired On, Folded, Funk, Get Back, Get Em Up, Get Off Where You Mad At, Get Wit Your Program, Go From The Shoulders, Hands, Hands & Feet, Knocked Down, Laminated, Leaked, Left Stankin', Leg Check, Let It Drip, Lit Up, Mean Mug, Molly Whopped, Mopped, Move Mean, Nut Up, On Sight, On Your Hat, On Your Helmet, One-Hitter-Quitter, Pop, Pump Fear, Roasted, Run Up, Scrape, See Me, Slumped, Smack, Smacked, Smash, Smoke, Smoked, Steppin' On S***, Stole On, Strike, Take Off, The Funk Is On, Whoride, Wit The S***, Woo Wop, Yank

Character Flaws & Negative Traits (53)
Actin' Funny, Bootsie, Bopper, Busta, Captain, Cat, Chester, Cold Piece Of Work, Dangler, Dope Fiend, Dry Snitch, Faggit, Fake, Faulty, Fluker, Hater, Hatin', High Power, Highside, Hoe Trusta, In The Way, J Cat, Mark, Noodle, Outta Pocket, P.H., Perpetrator, Player Hate, Player Hater, Pocket Watchin', Poodle, Punk Rock, Rathead, Ripper, Runner, Salt Your Game, Salted Out, Scary, Sellin', Side Bust, Side Buster, Skantless, Smirkish, Square, Sucka, Sucka S***, Sucka Standby, Suspect, Tellin', Toss Up, Weak Move, Weenie, Zark

Conversational Phrases (50)
4 Much, Ain't Even Cool, Ain't S***, All Geezus, All The S***, All To The Good, Alright Then, Be Smooth, Bet Not, But Now, Come-A-New, Cool On, Damn Near, Do The Damn Thang, Dry Run, Errythang, Finna, Hit Me On The Hip, I Ain't Trippin', I See You, In A Minute, In Me Not On Me, Is It Cool?, It's A Big Event, It's All Bad, It's All Good, It's Goin' Down, It's Nothin', It's Real Big, Keep It Funky, Knocked Out, Let That Go, Love, Love Yo Life, Mando, Mission, Nathan, Never That, Nodded, On Line, One Time, One Time For The One Time, Out Here, Tap In, The Longest, Tho, To The Neck, Tryna, Ugly, Young

Vehicles & Transportation (45)
4 15's, A1, Aunt Clara, Bap, Beat, Bend, Bounce Out, Bucket, Buss A B****, Dip, Donut, Dosin', Drop, Elroy, Fifty, Foot'n It, Ghostride, Gold Ones, Gold Thangs, L's, Mobby, Mobil, Mustard & Mayonnaise, Old School, On The Ground, Runnin', Scrape, Scraper, Scraper Bike, Servin', Squat, Stolo, Swang, Thangs, Tight Ones, Trophy, U-ey, Under Bucket, Under Mobby, Way-Way, Whip, Yikin', Yokin', Z's & V's, Zap

Local References & Geography (42)
Aunt Clara, B-Town, Bay Boy, Bay Luv, Baydestrian, City Situation, Deep East, E-1-4, E.P.A., E.S.O., Frisco, G-Thang, Hut, La Leezy, Lil Unda Spot, Liv Mo, N.S.O., Oaktown, Out The Way, S.F.C., San Fran, Sideshow, Strip, The "O", The Burg, The City, The Coli, The Flatlands, The Hyphy Movement, The Land, The North Pole, The Rich, The Stack, The Town, The West, Town Business, Turf, Unda Spot, V-Town, Valley Jo, W.S.O., Yay Area

Street Life & Hustle (39)
Active, Barz, Billy Doo, Bip, Blade, Bout That Action, Boy, Come Up, D-Boy, D-Boy Knot, Dangle, Do Ya Thug Thang, Factor, Flash, Front Street, Fronted Off, Game, Game Goofy, Game Laced, Game Recognize Game, Game Related, Game Tight, Gamed Up, Gank, Gangsta, Get Money, Grind, Grinding, Gutta, Hood, Hood Rich, Hustle, In The Field, Jackboy, Joog, On The Block, Pushin', Street, Trap

Relationships & Social (39)
Baby Girl, BD, Big Bruh, BM, Boo Thang, Brother, Bruh, Cuffed, Cuzzo, Day One, Folks, Homeboy, Homegirl, Kinfolk, Lady, Lil Bruh, Lil Mama, Main, My Boy, My Girl, My Hitta, My Mans, My Patna, O.G., Ol' Lady, Partner, Patna, Playboy, Potna, Road Dog, Round, Shawty, Solid, Squad, Thot, Wifey, Woadie, Yittadit, Young Life

Music & Sound (35)
4 15's, Banger, Bars, Barz, Beat, Bump, Dumb, Go Dumb, Go Stupid, Hyphy, Knock, Mac Dre, Mobb Music, Rap, Ridin', Scraper, Sideshow, Slap, Slapper, Smack, Sound, Speaker, Spittin', Stupid, Thizz, Thizzle, Thump, Thumper, Too Short, Trunk, Turn Up, Turnt, Turnt Up, Yay Yay, Yeee!

Positive Attributes & Praise (33)
A1, All Day, Baller, Boss, Bout It, Certified, Clean, Cold, Cutty, Decent, Fire, Fly, Fresh, G, Gamed Up, Gas, Go, Good, Hard, Heavy, Hittin', Hype, Legit, Lit, Official, Player, Real, Rider, Saucy, Smooth, Solid, Valid, Vicious

Fashion & Appearance (28)
Beat, Bling, Bummy, Clean, Drip, Drippin', Fit, Fitted, Fly, Fresh, Frontin', Gear, Gold, Grill, Ice, Icy, J's, Laced, Look, Pieced Up, Rockin', Sauce, Saucy, Shoe Game, Stunnas, Stuntin', Thang, Young

ABOUT THE PUBLISHER

First Class Media is an independent publishing house based in Oakland, California, dedicated to preserving and celebrating the rich cultural heritage of the Bay Area. We specialize in works that capture the authentic voices, stories, and language of our community.

CONNECT WITH US

thefirstclassmediagroup@gmail.com

www.firstclassmediagroup.com

www.ingramcontent.com/pod-product-compliance
Lightning Source LLC
Chambersburg PA
CBHW060451030426
42337CB00015B/1548